NIGHT
SKY

NIG
SKY

LIGHT

GILES SPARROW

SCHOLASTIC discover more™

How to discover more

This book is simple to use and enjoy, but knowing a little bit about how it works will help you discover more about the night sky and what interests you most about it. Have a great read!

How the pages work

The book is divided into chapters, such as **Watching the night sky**. Each chapter is made up of stand-alone spreads (double pages) that focus on specific topics.

What you can see
Use these panels as guides to spotting objects in the night sky yourself. Each panel shows you what to look for.

WHAT YOU CAN SEE

👁 Eye view | 🔭 Telescope

Viewing notes
Mars has a distinctive red color. It changes in brightness as our distance from it changes. Amateur telescopes can show dark and light patches on its surface.

Viewing icons
Discover how you can see things differently with your naked eye, binoculars, or a telescope.

Viewing notes
These notes tell you the features to look out for, such as the brightness, color, and size of a planet.

Introduction
Most spreads have a general introduction to the subject.

Fantastic facts
BIG text gives an amazing fact or quote!

Telescopes [Zooming in]

Use a telescope to view spectacular objects in the night sky, such as stars, planets, and even galaxies! Telescopes brighten and enlarge objects, so we can see much more with them than with the naked eye.

Galileo Galilei
By pointing a telescope at the night sky in the early 1600s, Galileo discovered that planets are round, that the Moon has mountains, and that the Sun, not Earth, is the center of the solar system.

Galileo Galilei
Italian astronomer Galileo used a telescope to show that Earth orbits the Sun.

Galileo's telescope **magnified by only 3 times!**

Invisible light
Light is a type of radiation (energy traveling through space). Many objects create radiation with more or less energy than visible light has. We can detect it using special telescopes.

Reflecting telescope
The reflecting telescope was invented by English scientist Isaac Newton around 1668. It collects light and bounces it toward an eyepiece lens to create a magnified image.

Viewfinder
This is used to point the larger telescope in the right direction

How it works
Light enters the telescope through a plate. The rays hit the primary mirror and are reflected to the secondary mirror. This mirror reflects the light back to the eyepiece, where the image is magnified and sent to the eye.

Eyepiece lens
A magnified image is created through this lens

Primary mirror
This curved mirror collects light.

Light enters
Plate

Secondary mirror
A smaller mirror reflects light back to the eyepiece.

Light enters

Refractor telescope
Lens-based telescopes are called refractors. They use lenses to refract (bend) light, directing it toward the eyepiece.

Viewfinder

How it works
Light enters through a large curved lens (called an objective lens) at the front of the telescope. Light rays meet at a point called the focus. As the rays spread apart again, the eyepiece collects them and magnifies an image.

Eyepiece
The eyepiece forms a magnified image.

Focus

Objective lens

Tripod stand

Binoculars
Binoculars are like two small telescopes joined together. They are a good tool for beginning astronomers.

Binoculars
Although they are not as powerful as a telescope, binoculars are portable and easy to use.

VISIBLE LIGHT

X-RAYS

RADIO WAVES

COMBINED VIEW

Four views of Centaurus A
The galaxy Centaurus A is shown in visible light, as an X-ray, and as a radio-wave image. At bottom, all three images are combined.

Digital companion book

Download your free, all-new digital book:

Light-Up Zodiac

Log on to
www.scholastic.com/ discovermore

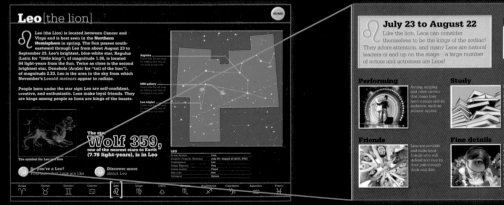

Features a star chart for every zodiac constellation.

Click to find out about people with your sign.

Warning boxes
Follow these guidelines to make sure that you don't damage your eyes when viewing the sky.

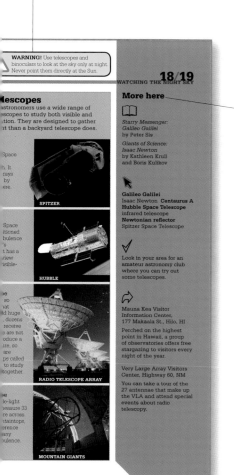

WARNING! Use telescopes and binoculars to look at the sky only at night. Never point them directly at the Sun.

18/19
WATCHING THE NIGHT SKY

elescopes

astronomers use a wide range of scopes to study both visible and tion. They are designed to gather t than a backyard telescope does.

Space

n. It
rays
by
ere.

SPITZER

Space
tioned
ulence
's
t has a
view
sible-

HUBBLE

e
go
at
d huge
dozens
are not
duce a
re, so
are
ps called
to study
together.

RADIO TELESCOPE ARRAY

e
le-light
easure 33
re across.
ntaintops,
erence
any
ulence.

MOUNTAIN GIANTS

More here

Starry Messenger: Galileo Galilei
by Peter Sis

Giants of Science: Isaac Newton
by Kathleen Krull and Boris Kulikov

Galileo Galilei
Isaac Newton **Centaurus A**
Hubble Space Telescope
infrared telescope
Newtonian reflector
Spitzer Space Telescope

✓ Look in your area for an amateur astronomy club where you can try out some telescopes.

Mauna Kea Visitor Information Center, 177 Makaala St., Hilo, HI
Perched on the highest point in Hawaii, a group of observatories offers free stargazing to visitors every night of the year.

Very Large Array Visitors Center, Highway 60, NM
You can take a tour of the 27 antennas that make up the VLA and attend special events about radio telescopy.

Spread types
Look out for different kinds of spreads. Constellation spreads include charts to help you spot groups of stars. Feature spreads on planets, the Moon, the Sun, and galaxies show more objects to look for and how the Universe works.

More here columns
This feature suggests books to read, words to look up on the Internet, places to visit, and things to do.

Key to symbols in More here columns

📖 *Suggested reading*

✓ *Do*

🖱 *Keywords for web searches*

➡ *Places to visit*

🔭 *View from afar*

▬ *Watch*

🔍 *Mini-glossary*

CONSTELLATION SPREAD

Discover the stories and unique stars of each of the major constellations. Use the charts to find star patterns in the sky.

FEATURE SPREAD

Feature spreads have detailed artwork and graphics, as well as fun and amazing facts.

This type of spread focuses on an extraordinary subject and includes images from NASA and the Hubble Space Telescope.

PHOTOGRAPHIC SPREAD

Glossary and index
The glossary explains words and phrases that might not be explained fully on the spreads or in the **More here** columns. The index can help you find pages throughout the book on which words and topics appear.

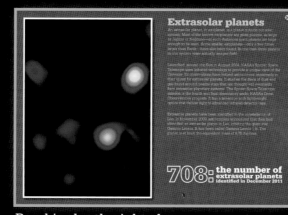

Read in-depth night sky encyclopedia entries.

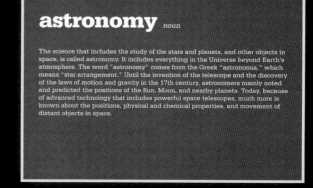

Look up night sky words.

Literacy consultant: Barbara Russ, 21st Century Community Learning Center Director for Winooski (Vermont) School District

Project editor: Dawn Bates

Project art editors: Emma Forge, Tom Forge

US editor: Elizabeth Krych

Art director: Bryn Walls

Managing editor: Miranda Smith

Managing production editor: Stephanie Anderson

Illustration: Tim Brown/Pikaia Imaging, Tim Loughhead/Precision Illustration

Cover designer: Natalie Godwin

DTP: John Goldsmid

Visual content editor: Dwayne Howard

Executive Director of Photography, Scholastic: Steve Diamond

"Anyone who does not ... gaze up and see the wonder ... of a dark night sky filled with countless stars loses a sense of their fundamental connectedness to the Universe."

—DR. BRIAN GREENE , COLUMBIA UNIVERSITY PHYSICIST

Library of Congress Cataloging-in-Publication Data Available

ISBN 978-0-545-38374-5

10 9 8 7 6 5 4 3 2 1   12 13 14 15 16

Printed in Singapore   46
First edition, May 2012

Scholastic is constantly working to lessen the environmental impact of our manufacturing processes. To view our industry-leading paper procurement policy, visit www.scholastic.com/paperpolicy.

Contents

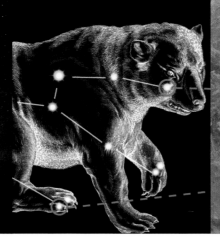

Northern lights

The breathtaking northern lights thrill sky watchers near Arctic regions. Often called the aurora borealis, this natural light display is created when solar wind particles (see page 36) collide with Earth's atmosphere. The resulting vibrant colors dance across the sky.

Galaxy crash

Galaxies are so big and have so much
gravitational pull that they can cluster
together and collide. This group of five
galaxies (two galaxies have merged to
look like one) is called Stephan's Quintet.
Although the bluish galaxy appears to
be on a collision course with the others,
in reality it is much closer to Earth.

Watchi
nigh

* Why do the stars appear to change positions?

* What will next be visible from Earth in 4530?

* What did Galileo discover?

The hour just after sunset is a great time to view the night sky. As day turns to night, you can see all kinds of objects with your naked eye, from nearby planets to distant stars.

Light pollution

As humans switch on electric lights after sunset, faint stars become hard to see. For the best sky views, try to get away from artificial lights, or block them out by positioning yourself behind a building.

Urban light
Electric lights can flood the night sky with artificial brightness.

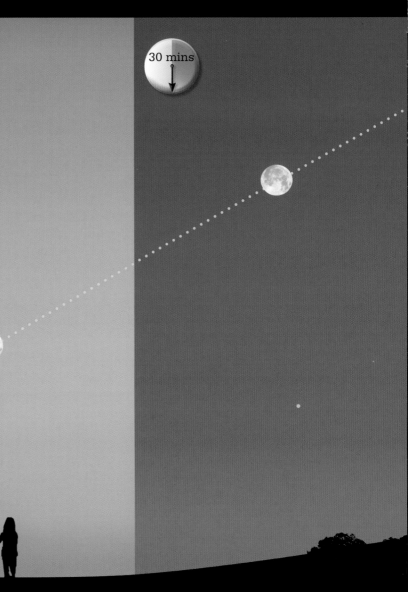

10 mins

20 mins

30 mins

Moon rising
The Moon's location in the sky changes nightly. At Full Moon, it rises as the Sun sets.

On the move
As the Earth spins, objects appear to move in a curved track across the sky.

Earth's shadow

Turn away from the sunset and look at the opposite side of the sky, just above the horizon. See a curved band of darkness beginning to rise? It's Earth's shadow, cast on the atmosphere.

Rising Moon

Around the time of the Full Moon (see page 69), the Moon will be rising as the Sun sets. The Moon's light is a faint reflection of the Sun's, but at night it becomes the brightest object in the sky.

Planet spotting

Venus, Mars, and Jupiter can all outshine the brightest stars. They may be the first starlike objects visible after sunset. You can tell a planet from a star because a planet does not twinkle.

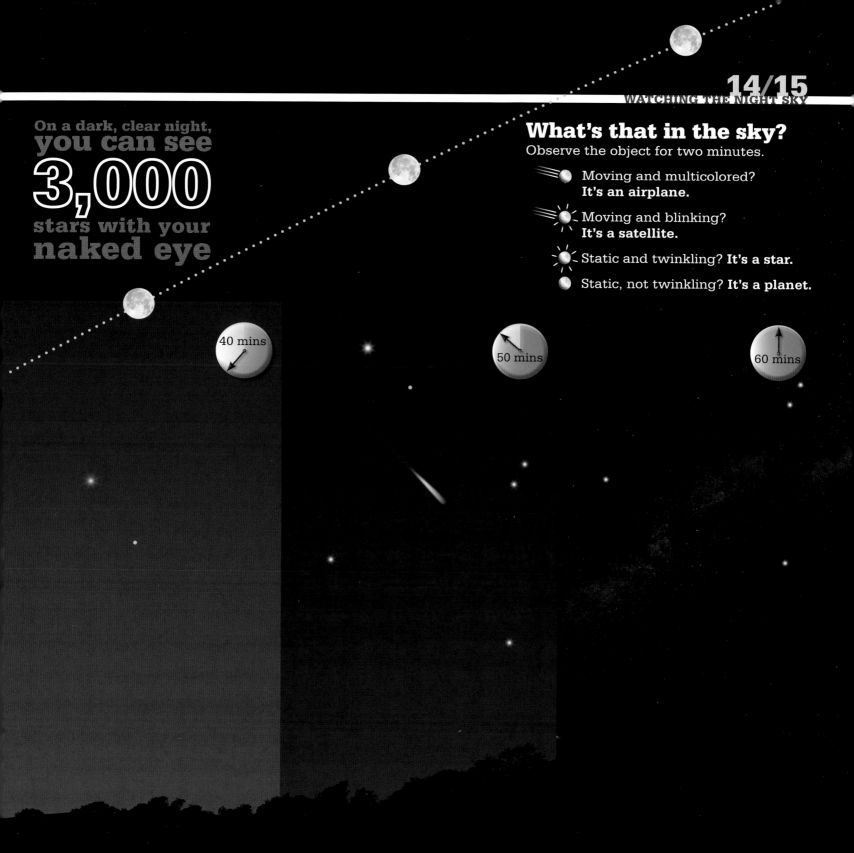

On a dark, clear night,
you can see
3,000
stars with your naked eye

What's that in the sky?
Observe the object for two minutes.

Moving and multicolored? **It's an airplane.**

Moving and blinking? **It's a satellite.**

Static and twinkling? **It's a star.**

Static, not twinkling? **It's a planet.**

40 mins

50 mins

60 mins

First stars
Eventually, the sky will be dark enough for the first stars to appear. They may twinkle and flicker as their light is bent and warped on its journey through Earth's turbulent air.

Shooting star
As the sky gets darker, you may see a streak of light. This is a meteor, or shooting star (see pages 32–33), a fragment of rock that burns up in a blaze of heat and light as it plunges from space into Earth's atmosphere.

The Milky Way
At full darkness, you can see a pale band of light—the Milky Way (see pages 94–95). By the end of the hour, it appears that the Moon and stars have moved, but in fact the Earth has spun beneath them.

You can see thousands of stars, and even some details on the Moon, with just your naked eye. To see farther and in greater focus, you will need binoculars or a telescope. An object's magnitude, or brightness, determines its visibility.

You can see an object up to **2.5 million** light-years away with the **naked eye**

Naked eye
With your eyes alone, you can see details on the Moon, nearby or especially bright stars, and even the closest galaxies.

What you can see
Faintest object visible is of magnitude 6 (see opposite page).

Naked-eye view of the Moon
You can make out vague dark and light patches.

Binoculars
Binoculars (see page 18) collect more light than your eyes do, so they can help you see fainter objects. They also magnify things so that you can see them in more detail.

What you can see
Faintest object visible is of magnitude 9.

Binocular view of the Moon
The patches form dark, smooth seas and bright, rocky highlands.

Backyard telescope
Telescopes (see pages 18–19) collect even more light than binoculars do, revealing the faintest objects and showing highly magnified, detailed images.

What you can see
Faintest object visible with a small telescope is around magnitude 12.

Telescopic view of the Moon
Through a telescope, you can see that the Moon is covered in mountains, craters (like this one), and smooth lava plains.

Try this!
To see faint objects with your naked eye, binoculars, or a telescope, use averted vision. Look slightly away from the object and watch it from the more sensitive edges of your eye.

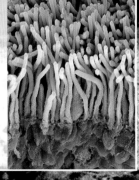

Central vision
The rod cells in the center of the eye (shown in pale brown, right) are good for color vision, but not for seeing faint detail.

WARNING! Use telescopes and binoculars to look at the sky only at night. Never point them directly at the Sun.

Use your naked eye to see:

Moon	250,000 miles (400,000 km) away
Saturn	900 million miles (1.5 billion km) away
Pleiades	400 light-years away
Andromeda galaxy	2.5 million light-years away

Pleiades
Many people can see seven stars with their naked eye in this cluster in Taurus (see pages 58–59).

Use your binoculars to see:

Asteroid Ceres	175 million miles (280 million km) away
Moons of Jupiter	372 million miles (600 million km) away
Uranus	1.7 billion miles (2.7 billion km) away
M101 galaxy	25 million light-years away

Jupiter and moons
Binoculars show Jupiter as a tiny disc orbited by the starlike points of its moons.

Use your telescope to see:

Neptune	2.7 billion miles (4.3 billion km) away
Ring Nebula	2,300 light-years away
M87 galaxy	54 million light-years away

Messier 87
This gigantic galaxy, visible with a telescope, contains a trillion stars.

📷 Photographing the sky
A camera can be a great way to see more detail and fainter objects. Long exposures allow cameras to soak up more light than our eyes can, increasing contrast and revealing the colors in starlight.

Seen with the naked eye
The Milky Way appears as an arc of faint white light stretching across the sky.

Seen with long exposure
A photograph can reveal colorful star clouds and the gas and dust between them.

How brightness is measured
Astronomers measure the brightness of objects in the sky on a scale called magnitude. Fainter objects have higher magnitudes. An object that is 1 unit of magnitude lower than another is about 2.5 times brighter.

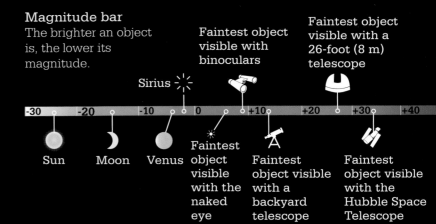

Magnitude bar
The brighter an object is, the lower its magnitude.

Sirius

Faintest object visible with binoculars

Faintest object visible with a 26-foot (8 m) telescope

-30 -20 -10 0 +10 +20 +30 +40

Sun Moon Venus

Faintest object visible with the naked eye

Faintest object visible with a backyard telescope

Faintest object visible with the Hubble Space Telescope

Telescopes [Zooming in]

Use a telescope to view spectacular objects in the night sky, such as stars, planets, and even galaxies! Telescopes brighten and enlarge objects, so we can see much more with them than with the naked eye.

Galileo Galilei

By pointing a telescope at the night sky in the early 1600s, Galileo discovered that planets are round, that the Moon has mountains, and that the Sun, not Earth, is the center of the solar system.

Galileo Galilei
Italian astronomer Galileo used a telescope to show that Earth orbits the Sun.

Reflecting telescope

The reflecting telescope was invented by English scientist Isaac Newton around 1668. It collects light and bounces it toward an eyepiece lens to create a magnified image.

Viewfinder
This is used to point the larger telescope in the right direction.

How it works
Light enters the telescope through a plate. The rays hit the primary mirror and are reflected to the secondary mirror. This mirror reflects the light back to the eyepiece, where the image is magnified and sent to the eye.

Eyepiece lens
A magnified image is created through this lens.

Primary mirror
This curved mirror collects light.

Light enters

Plate

Secondary mirror
A smaller mirror reflects light back to the eyepiece.

Galileo's telescope **magnified by only 3 times!**

Light enters

Refractor telescope

Lens-based telescopes are called refractors. They use lenses to refract (bend) light, directing it toward the eyepiece.

How it works
Light enters through a large curved lens (called an objective lens) at the front of the telescope. Light rays meet at a point called the focus. As the rays spread apart again, the eyepiece collects them and magnifies an image.

Viewfinder

Focus

Eyepiece
The eyepiece forms a magnified image.

Tripod stand

Objective lens

Binoculars

Binoculars are like two small telescopes joined together. They are a good tool for beginning astronomers.

Binoculars
Although they are not as powerful as a telescope, binoculars are portable and easy to use.

WARNING! Use telescopes and binoculars to look at the sky only at night. Never point them directly at the Sun.

Invisible light

Light is a type of radiation (energy traveling through space). Many objects create radiation with more or less energy than visible light has. We can detect it using special telescopes.

VISIBLE LIGHT

X-RAYS

RADIO WAVES

COMBINED VIEW

Four views of Centaurus A
The galaxy Centaurus A is shown in visible light, as an X-ray, and as a radio-wave image. At bottom, all three images are combined.

Supertelescopes

Professional astronomers use a wide range of high-tech telescopes to study both visible and invisible radiation. They are designed to gather a lot more light than a backyard telescope does.

Spitzer
NASA's Spitzer Space Telescope orbits high above Earth. It detects infrared rays that are blocked by Earth's atmosphere.

SPITZER

Hubble
NASA's Hubble Space Telescope is positioned far above the turbulence caused by Earth's atmosphere, so it has a clearer, sharper view than any other visible-light telescope.

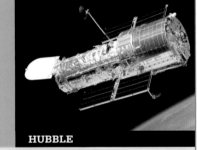

HUBBLE

Radio telescope
Radio waves are so large and faint that astronomers build huge receiving dishes, dozens of feet across, to receive them. Even these are not big enough to produce a really sharp picture, so radio telescopes are gathered in groups called arrays, designed to study the same object together.

RADIO TELESCOPE ARRAY

Dome telescope
The largest visible-light telescopes can measure 33 feet (10 m) or more across. Located on mountaintops, they avoid interference from clouds and any atmospheric turbulence.

MOUNTAIN GIANTS

More here

Starry Messenger: Galileo Galilei
by Peter Sís

Giants of Science: Isaac Newton
by Kathleen Krull and Boris Kulikov

Galileo Galilei
Isaac Newton **Centaurus A**
Hubble Space Telescope
infrared telescope
Newtonian reflector
Spitzer Space Telescope

Look in your area for an amateur astronomy club where you can try out some telescopes.

Mauna Kea Visitor Information Center, 177 Makaala St., Hilo, HI

Perched on the highest point in Hawaii, a group of observatories offers free stargazing to visitors every night of the year.

Very Large Array Visitors Center, Highway 60, NM

You can take a tour of the 27 antennae that make up the VLA and attend special events about radio telescopy.

View from Earth

Looking up into the night sky, it seems as if we're surrounded by a huge shell that has the Sun, Moon, stars, and planets moving around on it. This imaginary sphere can help explain how we see the stars.

Early theories

Ancient astronomers thought that the celestial sphere was physically real, and that the Sun, Moon, and planets moved on smaller spheres closer to Earth.

Atlas holding the world

The legendary giant Atlas was forced to separate Earth from the sky. He is famously shown carrying a celestial sphere with the constellations shown on it.

Celestial sphere

Since ancient times, astronomers have imagined that the stars are projected on a celestial, or "heavenly," sphere. This model gives a standard depiction of the position of stars, and explains why we see stars differently at different times and places.

Star

Star

Coordinate grid
Astronomers mark the sphere with lines so that they can pinpoint the positions of space objects.

Surface of sphere

Celestial pole
As Earth rotates, the celestial sphere seems to spin around fixed points above the North and South Poles.

Different distances of stars
Remember that the celestial sphere is just a useful imaginary idea—in reality, most stars are at different distances from one another in space, not on one fixed plane.

Ecliptic
Over one year, the Sun follows the ecliptic path around the sky. It passes through the constellations of the zodiac (see page 28). The planets also stay close to this path.

Celestial equator
This line, directly above Earth's Equator, splits the sky into northern and southern halves. These two halves are called hemispheres.

Sun
As Earth moves around the Sun, the Sun changes its location on the sphere.

Looking inside
In this cutaway illustration, you can see how Earth fits in the center of the celestial sphere.

The celestial sphere spins once every
23 hours, 56 minutes

Our view of the night sky

From any place on Earth, we can see half the celestial sphere at a time. Earth's rotation shows us different parts of the sky through the night, but some areas are forever below the horizon, and we can see them only by changing our location.

Worldwide view
This diagram shows three different stargazers' views of the sky: one person in San Francisco, one in Turkey, and one in Argentina.

North celestial pole
The celestial pole always lies in the same direction.

Stationary stars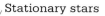

Changing position
Locations on the same level on Earth see the same areas of sky as Earth rotates.

VIEW FROM SAN FRANCISCO

VIEW FROM TURKEY

Earth

Celestial sphere

Rotating planet
Earth's daily rotation carries us on a circular path around its axis, so different parts of the sphere are overhead at different times of night.

Spinning sky

As Earth rotates, the stars trace curving paths across the sky. They rise in the east and set in the west, making circles around the celestial pole.

Half the sky
The bulk of Earth beneath our feet always blocks half the celestial sphere from view.

Southern view
From a different latitude—for instance, in the Southern Hemisphere—we see a different area of the sky.

South celestial pole

VIEW FROM ARGENTINA

Celestial circles
Long-exposure photos capture the motion of the stars around Polaris.

Looking at the night sky for patterns of stars, called constellations, is a fun and rewarding part of astronomy. One of the most famous constellations in the northern sky is the Great Bear, also called Ursa Major (in Latin). Within its outline is the group of stars known as the Big Dipper.

88 : the official number of **constellations that have been** cataloged by modern **astronomers**

Seven stars
The seven brightest stars of Ursa Major form an asterism, a simple pattern that is smaller than the constellation as a whole.

Large constellation
Ursa Major's fainter stars spread across a large area of sky, making the Great Bear the third-largest constellation.

North and south

Some constellations are easier to identify than others because of their shape. The Great Bear is a complicated shape and takes some imagination to see (see opposite page). The Southern Cross (Crux Australis), though, is an easy shape to spot in a starry sky.

The Great Bear
The pattern of Ursa Major resembles a bear. Parts of its body and tail, shown in yellow, form another pattern, the Big Dipper.

The Southern Cross
The most famous constellation in the southern skies, the Southern Cross, is also the smallest constellation of all.

What shape do you see?

While the positions of the stars have barely moved over thousands of years, different cultures have seen the same groups of stars in different ways. The ancient Greeks named 48 constellations, most based on mythological figures. Ancient Egyptian and medieval Arabic astronomers recognized different names and shapes.

Celestial globe
This beautiful 1878 globe is decorated with elaborate figures. It illustrates constellations such as Leo, the Lion, and Hydra, the Water Snake.

Leo
This star pattern forms the image of a crouching lion (see pages 46–47).

Hydra
The largest constellation, Hydra, is shown as a water snake.

Sky in reverse
The pictures on this globe are reversed, compared to our view from Earth.

The Big Dipper
American stargazers see the seven brightest stars in Ursa Major as a ladle.

The Plow
European stargazers usually compare the same seven stars to an old-fashioned plow.

Look for a constellation

The best way to find your way around the sky is to learn a few key star patterns, such as the ones in Chapter 2. Then use the large star maps on pages 24–29 to see how they relate to other constellations and to the entire sky.

Mizar
The middle star of the bear's tail has a faint nearby companion named Alcor.

Dark skies
To see a constellation clearly, choose a dark night and avoid light pollution (see page 14).

Mythical figures
To the ancient Greeks, the Great Bear represented Callisto, a beautiful woman who was turned into a bear by the jealous goddess Hera.

Modern star maps
Today, astronomers define 88 constellations—areas of sky around the traditional patterns. In this system, every object in the sky is placed in a constellation.

Northern skies [Star map]

The northern half of the celestial sphere (see page 20), the region of sky familiar to European and Asian astronomers, was mapped with many constellations long ago. They are positioned around the north celestial pole, marked by the star Polaris.

NORTHERN HEMISPHERE

Northern Hemisphere

This map shows the sky as it appears if you stand at the North Pole looking straight up. These stars can be seen at various times of year from the Northern Hemisphere. But if you are south of the Equator, the stars that are closest to the North Pole are always out of sight.

Stars and other objects

This map shows all the stars visible to the naked eye in this part of the sky, as well as some bright and interesting deep-sky objects—star clusters, gaseous nebulae, and galaxies.

A different view

The constellations on the big chart come mostly from a list of 48 star patterns written down by European astronomers in the second century CE. Chinese astronomers saw the sky differently, making different constellations out of smaller groups of stars.

Leo
see pages 46–47

North Pole

Orion
see pages 40–41

Celestial equator

Ecliptic

Taurus
see pages 58–59

North Star, Polaris

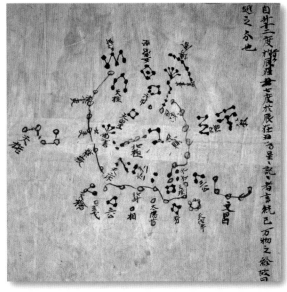

Ancient Chinese map
This map from around 650 CE shows a Chinese astronomer's view of star patterns in the Northern Hemisphere.

SEXTANS · LEO · CANCER · LEO MINOR · M44 · CANIS MINOR · Procyon · GEMINI · THE BIG DIPPER · LYNX · MONOCEROS · M35 · M36 · AURIGA · M38 · CAMELOPARDALIS · Capella · PERSEUS · Polaris · Betelgeuse · ORION · Aldebaran · TAURUS · HYADES · PLEIADES · M34 · CASSIOPEIA · M31 · TRIANGULUM · ARIES · CETUS · PISCES

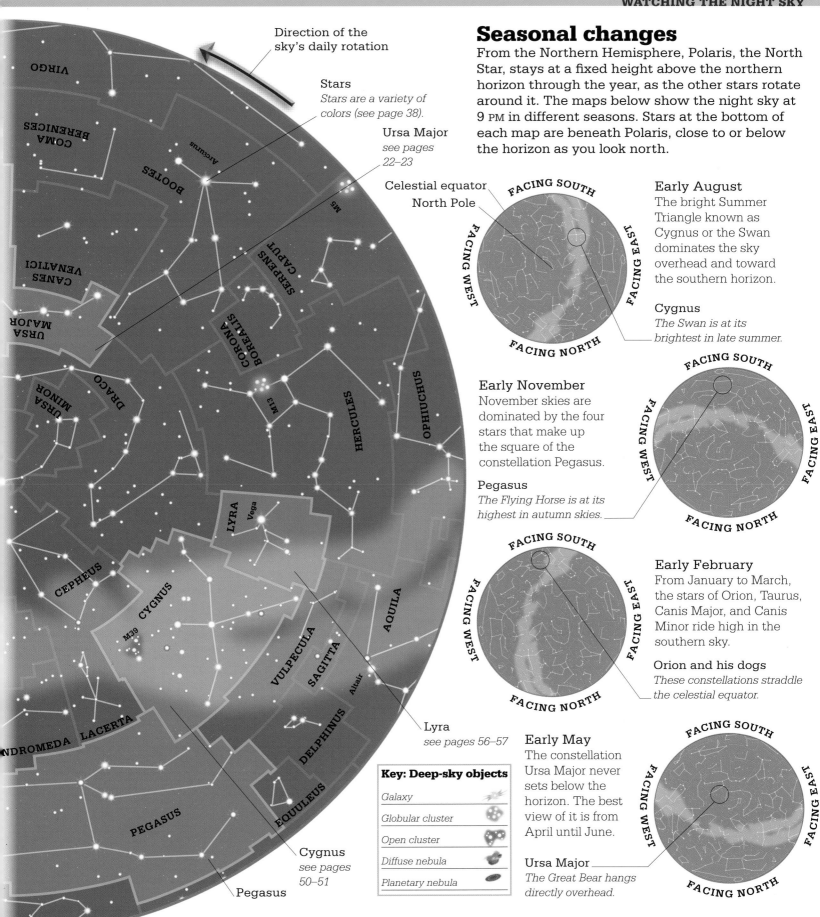

Direction of the sky's daily rotation

Stars
Stars are a variety of colors (see page 38).

Ursa Major
see pages 22–23

Celestial equator

North Pole

Lyra
see pages 56–57

Cygnus
see pages 50–51

Pegasus

Key: Deep-sky objects

Galaxy	
Globular cluster	
Open cluster	
Diffuse nebula	
Planetary nebula	

Seasonal changes

From the Northern Hemisphere, Polaris, the North Star, stays at a fixed height above the northern horizon through the year, as the other stars rotate around it. The maps below show the night sky at 9 PM in different seasons. Stars at the bottom of each map are beneath Polaris, close to or below the horizon as you look north.

Early August
The bright Summer Triangle known as Cygnus or the Swan dominates the sky overhead and toward the southern horizon.

Cygnus
The Swan is at its brightest in late summer.

Early November
November skies are dominated by the four stars that make up the square of the constellation Pegasus.

Pegasus
The Flying Horse is at its highest in autumn skies.

Early February
From January to March, the stars of Orion, Taurus, Canis Major, and Canis Minor ride high in the southern sky.

Orion and his dogs
These constellations straddle the celestial equator.

Early May
The constellation Ursa Major never sets below the horizon. The best view of it is from April until June.

Ursa Major
The Great Bear hangs directly overhead.

Southern skies [Star map]

The constellations that lie to the south of the celestial equator (see page 28) have a wide range of ages, sizes, and brightnesses. Some of them are the most brilliant in the sky, while others—particularly those around the south celestial pole—are the most obscure.

SOUTHERN HEMISPHERE

What you can see

This map shows the sky as it would appear if you stood at the South Pole and looked straight up. Many of these stars are also visible from the Northern Hemisphere, but the farther north you go, the farther the south celestial pole sinks out of sight.

Mapping the sky
This map shows all the stars visible to the naked eye in this part of the sky, as well as some bright and interesting deep-sky objects—star clusters, nebulae, and galaxies.

Southern figures
The constellations of the Southern Hemisphere depict a variety of mythical figures, animals, tools, and inventions.

Discovering constellations

Parts of the southern sky closest to the celestial equator were known to the ancient Greeks and included in their original list of 48 constellations. It was the 1500s, however, before the first Europeans—sailors—saw the sky around the south celestial pole.

Nicolas Louis de Lacaille
This French astronomer cataloged nearly 10,000 southern stars in the 1750s. He named 14 new constellations in the process.

Centaurus

Scorpius
see pages 52–53

Crux

Celestial equator

Ecliptic

Sagittarius
see pages 42–43

No South Star
Unlike in the Northern Hemisphere, there is no bright star close to the south celestial pole.

VIRGO · CORVUS · CENTAURUS · LIBRA · LUPUS · CIRCINUS · CRUX · Acrux · Alpha Centauri · MUSCA · OPHIUCHUS · M4 · Antares · SCORPIUS · M6 · NORMA · TRIANGULUM AUSTRALE · APUS · SERPENS CAUDA · M20 · M7 · CORONA AUSTRALIS · ARA · TELESCOPIUM · PAVO · OCTANS · M24 · M25 · SCUTUM · M28 · M22 · SMC · M11 · SAGITTARIUS · TUCAN · INDUS · AQUILA · MICROSCOPIUM · CAPRICORNUS · GRUS · PISCIS AUSTRINUS · AQUARIUS · Fomalhaut · Spica

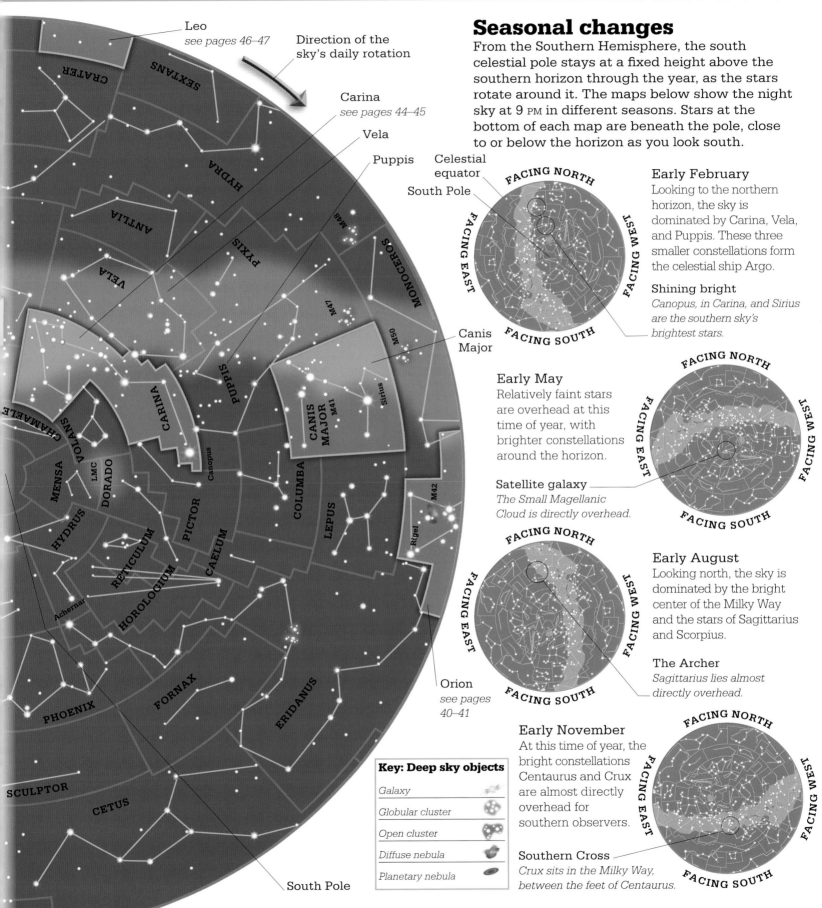

Leo
see pages 46–47

Direction of the sky's daily rotation

Carina
see pages 44–45

Vela

Puppis

Celestial equator

South Pole

Canis Major

Orion
see pages 40–41

South Pole

CRATER

SEXTANS

HYDRA

ANTLIA

PYXIS

VELA

MONOCEROS

M46

M47

M50

M48

PUPPIS

CARINA

CHAMAELE

VOLANS

MENSA

LMC

DORADO

HYDRUS

RETICULUM

HOROLOGIUM

PICTOR

CAELUM

COLUMBA

LEPUS

CANIS MAJOR

M41

Sirius

M42

Rigel

Canopus

Achernar

PHOENIX

FORNAX

ERIDANUS

SCULPTOR

CETUS

Key: Deep sky objects

Galaxy	
Globular cluster	
Open cluster	
Diffuse nebula	
Planetary nebula	

Seasonal changes

From the Southern Hemisphere, the south celestial pole stays at a fixed height above the southern horizon through the year, as the stars rotate around it. The maps below show the night sky at 9 PM in different seasons. Stars at the bottom of each map are beneath the pole, close to or below the horizon as you look south.

FACING NORTH

FACING WEST

FACING EAST

FACING SOUTH

Early February
Looking to the northern horizon, the sky is dominated by Carina, Vela, and Puppis. These three smaller constellations form the celestial ship Argo.

Shining bright
Canopus, in Carina, and Sirius are the southern sky's brightest stars.

FACING NORTH

FACING WEST

FACING EAST

FACING SOUTH

Early May
Relatively faint stars are overhead at this time of year, with brighter constellations around the horizon.

Satellite galaxy
The Small Magellanic Cloud is directly overhead.

FACING NORTH

FACING WEST

FACING EAST

FACING SOUTH

Early August
Looking north, the sky is dominated by the bright center of the Milky Way and the stars of Sagittarius and Scorpius.

The Archer
Sagittarius lies almost directly overhead.

FACING NORTH

FACING WEST

FACING EAST

FACING SOUTH

Early November
At this time of year, the bright constellations Centaurus and Crux are almost directly overhead for southern observers.

Southern Cross
Crux sits in the Milky Way, between the feet of Centaurus.

Equatorial skies [Star map]

The sky map is divided equally into northern and southern hemispheres by the celestial equator. Around the equator are the 12 zodiac constellations, which some people relate to their birthdays.

View of both hemispheres

Except at the poles, stargazers in one hemisphere can always see some stars in the other hemisphere. The closer to the Equator you are, the more of the other hemisphere's stars you can see.

EQUATORIAL SKIES

Star map
This map shows the stars around the celestial equator, visible from both hemispheres.

Direction of the sky's daily rotation

Cygnus
see pages 50–51

Lyra
see pages 56–57

Ursa Major
see pages 22–23

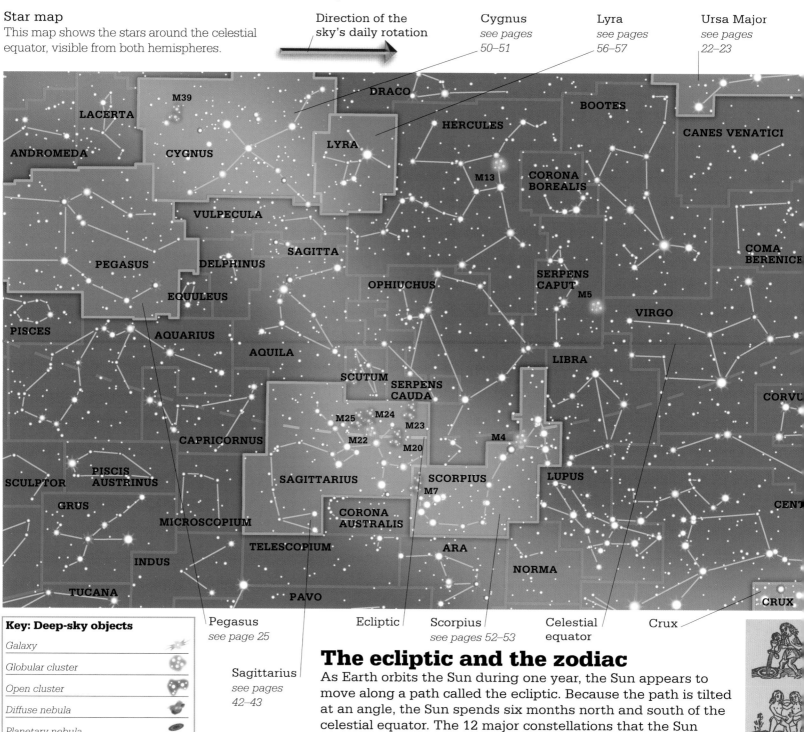

Pegasus
see page 25

Ecliptic

Scorpius
see pages 52–53

Celestial equator

Crux

Sagittarius
see pages 42–43

Key: Deep-sky objects

Galaxy	
Globular cluster	
Open cluster	
Diffuse nebula	
Planetary nebula	

The ecliptic and the zodiac

As Earth orbits the Sun during one year, the Sun appears to move along a path called the ecliptic. Because the path is tilted at an angle, the Sun spends six months north and south of the celestial equator. The 12 major constellations that the Sun passes through each year form a band called the zodiac.

Mapping the skies

The earliest star charts and catalogs date from ancient Iraq, around 1200 BCE. Many of these were passed on to Greek astronomers such as Ptolemy, who wrote a summary of ancient astronomy called the *Almagest* around 150 CE.

Ptolemy (ca. 100–170 CE)
His *Almagest* includes a list of 48 constellations of northern and equatorial skies.

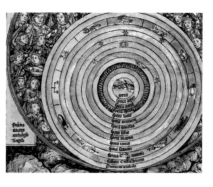

Ptolemaic universe
Ptolemy believed that the Earth was the center of the Universe, with the Sun, Moon, planets, and stars circling around it.

Leo
see pages 46–47

Canis Minor
see page 40

Orion
see pages 40–41

Taurus
see pages 58–59

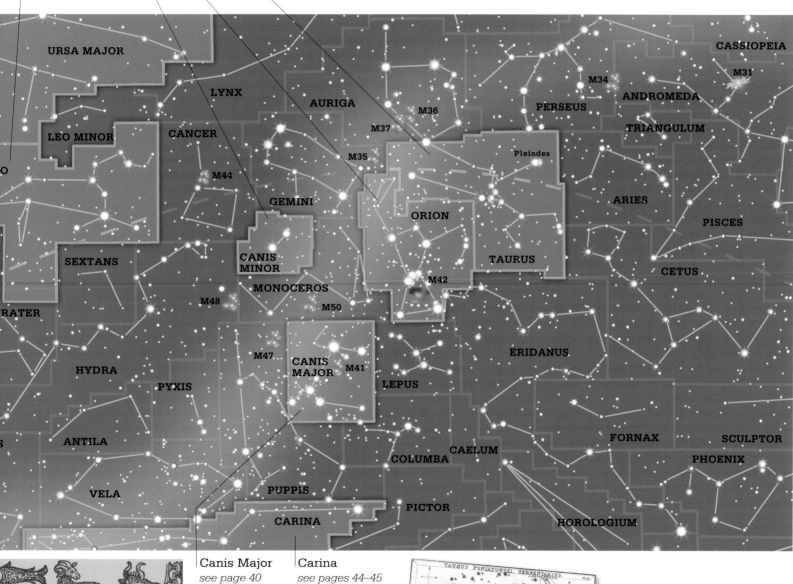

URSA MAJOR
LYNX
LEO MINOR
CANCER
SEXTANS
CRATER
HYDRA
PYXIS
ANTILA
VELA
AURIGA
M37
M35
M44
GEMINI
CANIS MINOR
MONOCEROS
M48
M50
M47
CANIS MAJOR
M41
LEPUS
PUPPIS
CARINA
PICTOR
COLUMBA
CAELUM
M36
M34
ORION
M42
TAURUS
ERIDANUS
FORNAX
PHOENIX
HOROLOGIUM
SCULPTOR
CETUS
PISCES
ARIES
TRIANGULUM
ANDROMEDA
M31
CASSIOPEIA
PERSEUS
Pleiades

Canis Major
see page 40

Carina
see pages 44–45

Signs of the zodiac

Whichever constellation the Sun is in at the time you are born is called your zodiac sign. Some people believe that your sign can influence your personality.

The 13th sign of the zodiac?

Each December, the Sun spends 18 days in the constellation of Ophiuchus, the Serpent Bearer, but Ophiuchus isn't counted as an official zodiac sign.

Hale-Bopp over Hawaii

Comets are chunks of rock and ice that orbit the Sun. A rise in temperature as they approach the Sun triggers activity. In 1997, the stunning Hale-Bopp, shown here streaking above the clouds over Hawaii, was one of the brightest comets ever seen. It was visible for several months and will next be seen from Earth in 4530.

Meteors [Shooting stars]

Watch the sky on a clear night, and you might spot a fast-moving streak across the darkness. It could be a meteor, commonly known as a shooting star, created as space debris burns up in the atmosphere.

Meteor shower
Dozens or even hundreds of shooting stars per hour appear to come from the same part of the sky during a meteor shower. The heaviest showers, with thousands of meteors per hour, are called meteor storms.

A link to comets
Giovanni Schiaparelli, a 19th-century astronomer, realized that meteor streams are spread out along the orbits of comets. He concluded that meteor showers are produced when comets decay.

Giovanni Schiaparelli
This Italian astronomer discovered the link between meteors and comets.

Meteorites
Among the dust and debris of the solar system are bigger chunks of rock. Those that are large enough to travel through Earth's atmosphere without burning up are called meteorites once they reach Earth's surface. Meteorites range in size from rocks only a few inches long to rare asteroids (see page 88) that can be many miles wide.

Canyon Diablo
This meteorite landed in Canyon Diablo, Arizona.

Life of a meteorite
As a meteor hits Earth's atmosphere, it begins to heat up. Many meteors burn away completely, but the occasional large rock makes it through the atmosphere and slams into Earth's surface, sometimes causing a huge crater. It is now known as a meteorite.

1 Approaching Earth
A meteor may meet our planet head-on at speeds of thousands of miles per hour, or catch up with it much more slowly.

2 Entering the atmosphere
Friction with air molecules in the upper atmosphere heats the meteor until it is red hot and starts to glow.

Space junk

Most meteors and meteorites are natural debris left over from the birth of our solar system. But in the past 50 years, human space explorers have been filling space with garbage, from flecks of paint to broken satellites. Some of that trash reenters the atmosphere and burns up, but a lot hangs around in Earth's orbit.

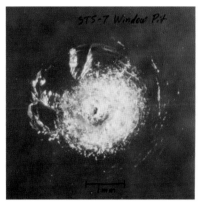

Damage
NASA's space shuttle *Challenger* suffered occasional damage from collisions with fragments of space junk. This hole in its window was made by a fleck of paint.

1,000
tons of space debris
land on Earth each year

3 Fireball!
The largest and brightest meteors are called fireballs. They are most likely to hit Earth.

4 Impact craters
Rare meteorites 30 feet (10 m) across or more can gouge craters out of the Earth, but most meteorite impacts are much smaller.

5 Death of the dinosaurs
An enormous meteorite impact, 65 million years ago in present-day Mexico, plunged Earth into a climate crisis that may have wiped out the dinosaurs.

Search the S

* Why does the Sun have spots?

* Where in the night sky can you see a horse's head?

* What is a red giant?

ing for
tars

The Sun [Our closest star]

An exploding ball of superhot gas 93 million miles (150 million km) away, the Sun is the ultimate source of all our heat and light. Its close proximity to Earth makes the Sun the only star that astronomers can study up close.

Surface features
The Sun's surface constantly changes. Rising columns of hot gas give it a grainy pattern, and its powerful magnetic field creates sunspots and violent solar flares.

Surface of the Sun
The Sun is a ball of gas that gets denser toward its center. Its visible surface is a layer called the photosphere, which marks the boundary between the dense, opaque interior and the thinner, transparent outer layers. The gases of the photosphere are heated to around 9,600°F (5,500°C), and they glow an incandescent yellow-white.

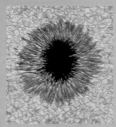

Sunspots
Even cooler parts of the surface are around 5,500°F (3,000°C). They look dark because they are cool compared to their surroundings.

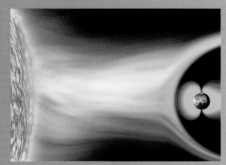

Solar wind
A constant stream of particles blows away from the Sun at hundreds of miles per second. This wind is deflected by the magnetic fields of planets such as Earth.

Lighting up the sky
Particles from the Sun's wind are channeled into the atmosphere above Earth. This creates surprising and beautiful lights—the aurora borealis and aurora australis (see pages 8–9).

Visible surface
Known as the photosphere, the visible surface of the Sun is actually a layer of mist 600 miles (1,000 km) deep. The surface just appears solid because it is so far away from Earth.

Solar flare
Sudden changes to the Sun's shifting magnetic field can release huge amounts of energy. This energy heats up gas that escapes from the Sun, causing solar flares.

332,950 Earths = the weight of 1 Sun

36/37
SEARCHING FOR THE STARS

Convective zone
Hot gas rises and is released through this zone.

Structure of the Sun

The Sun has three main layers: the core, the radiative zone, and the convective zone. High-energy radiation is produced in the core, escapes into the radiative zone, bounces around there, and loses energy. At the base of the convective zone, the radiation heats up gas, which rises and releases energy again as heat and light from the Sun's surface.

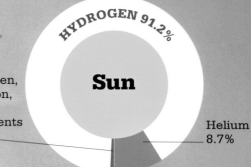

HYDROGEN 91.2%

Sun

Oxygen, carbon, other elements 0.1%

Helium 8.7%

The Sun's composition
The Sun's chemical makeup is dominated by the simplest and most lightweight elements in the Universe—hydrogen and helium.

Radiative zone
Radiation bounces around in dense gas for thousands of years.

Core

Energy source

The extreme temperatures (27 million°F / 15 million°C) and pressures at the heart of the Sun force the nuclei of its hydrogen atoms together, creating helium. This process, called nuclear fusion, releases huge amounts of energy.

Convective zone
Energy is absorbed to heat gas at the base of this zone.

Sunspots
These come and go in 11-year cycles.

Nuclear fusion research
This device is being used to assess nuclear fusion as a renewable source of energy. As no nuclear fusion plants have been built yet, the Sun is still the best at creating energy from it.

Surface
Gas releases energy, cools, and sinks.

Variety of stars [So colorful]

A careful look at the night sky reveals a huge range in the colors and brightnesses of stars. How are stars formed, and what causes the differences between them?

Multicolored sky

Stars look white at first glance, but they are actually many different colors. A star's color depends on its average surface temperature and the energy of the light it emits. An iron bar heated in a furnace glows red at first but blue when it is hottest; likewise, the hottest stars shine blue.

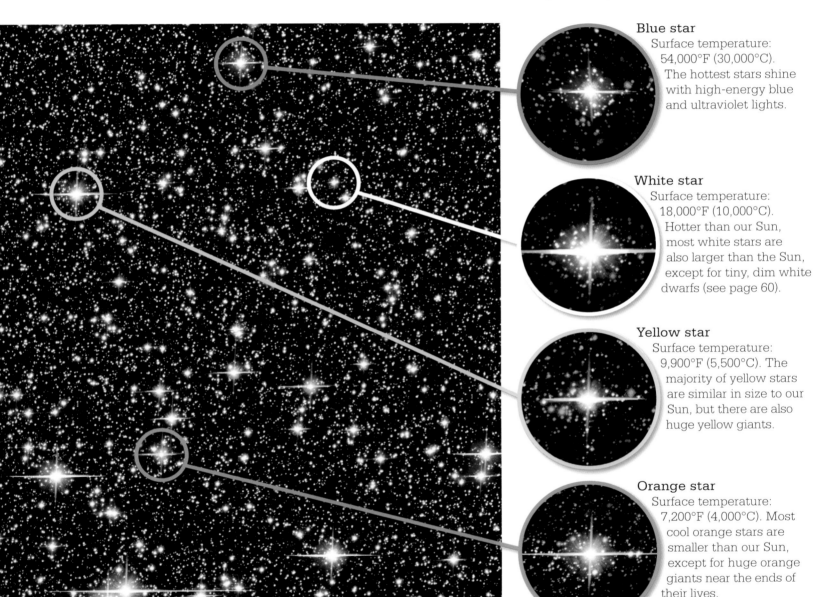

Colorful wonders
The star clouds of the constellation Sagittarius (see pages 42–43) lie near the center of the Milky Way. This superb Hubble Space Telescope image shows countless stars of different colors and brightnesses.

Blue star
Surface temperature: 54,000°F (30,000°C). The hottest stars shine with high-energy blue and ultraviolet lights.

White star
Surface temperature: 18,000°F (10,000°C). Hotter than our Sun, most white stars are also larger than the Sun, except for tiny, dim white dwarfs (see page 60).

Yellow star
Surface temperature: 9,900°F (5,500°C). The majority of yellow stars are similar in size to our Sun, but there are also huge yellow giants.

Orange star
Surface temperature: 7,200°F (4,000°C). Most cool orange stars are smaller than our Sun, except for huge orange giants near the ends of their lives.

Red star

Surface temperature: 5,400°F (3,000°C). Most red stars are small and insignificant. The brightest red stars in Earth's sky are all enormous but distant dying stars—red giants.

Size of a star

The size of a star is related to its color and its brightness. Stars range in size from red dwarfs to blue giants, with our Sun lying somewhere in the middle of these two extremes. But when a star is dying, it increases in size and glows red, too.

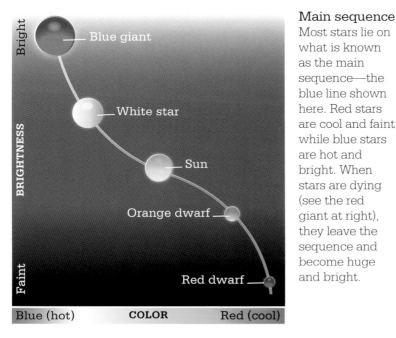

Bright

BRIGHTNESS

Faint

Blue giant

White star

Sun

Orange dwarf

Red dwarf

Blue (hot)   COLOR   Red (cool)

Main sequence
Most stars lie on what is known as the main sequence—the blue line shown here. Red stars are cool and faint, while blue stars are hot and bright. When stars are dying (see the red giant at right), they leave the sequence and become huge and bright.

Weight of a star

When astronomers find two stars orbiting a common point in space, they can work out the relative weights of each star. These weights reveal a pattern—dim red stars are small and light, while brilliant blue ones are larger and heavier.

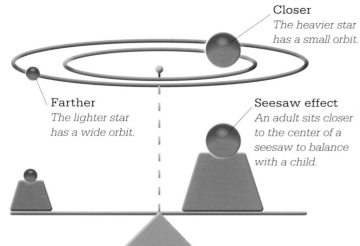

Closer
The heavier star has a small orbit.

Farther
The lighter star has a wide orbit.

Seesaw effect
An adult sits closer to the center of a seesaw to balance with a child.

A balancing act
When an adult and a child sit on a seesaw, the heavier adult has to sit closer to the center to keep it in balance. The same principle applies when two stars orbit a common point—the blue star orbiting nearer the middle must be heavier then the red star.

Life cycle of a star

By comparing the brightnesses, colors, sizes, and weights of stars, and adding what we know from studies of the Sun, astronomers can map out the life story of a typical star.

1 Star birth
Stars are born from collapsing gas clouds that grow large and dense enough to begin nuclear reactions (see page 40).

2 Star cluster
Although stars within a single cluster form around the same time, the rate at which they age depends on their weights (see page 42).

3 Main sequence
Stars spend most of their lives shining due to the nuclear fusion of hydrogen. During this period, the size of a star is related to its color and brightness (see page 47).

4 Red giant
When a star runs out of hydrogen, it burns other elements, growing brighter and redder regardless of its weight (see page 53).

5 Death of a star

Planetary nebula
Light stars puff off their outer layers in shells (see page 56).

Supernova
The heaviest stars die in violent explosions (see page 58).

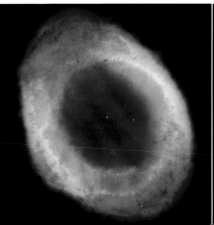
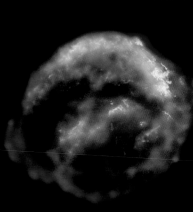

Orion [The Hunter]

One of the brightest and best-known constellations in the entire night sky is Orion. It is exceptional because parts of it can be seen from both the North and South Poles.

Constellation FACT FILE

Common name	The Hunter
Abbreviation	Ori
Visible from	Worldwide
Best time to see	December to March, after sunset
Brightest star	Rigel

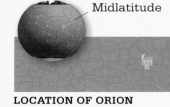

Midlatitude

LOCATION OF ORION

Origins

Ancient Greeks saw the pattern as the mighty hunter Orion. With his dogs Canis Major and Canis Minor, he faced the charging bull Taurus (see pages 58–59).

Orion confronts Taurus with a club.

Orion
This engraving shows how you can see the mythical figure of Orion in the stars.

> **"No other constellation more accurately represents the figure of a man"**
> —Germanicus Caesar (15 BCE–19 CE)

Orion's highlights

Many of Orion's interesting objects are quite close to one another. Its various nebulae, which are clouds of gas and dust, form parts of the huge Orion Molecular Cloud. Many of its bright stars were born from this cloud.

Orion's sword
A chain of bright young stars to the south of Orion's belt forms his sword.

Great Nebula
In the middle of the sword lies the Great Orion Nebula, a place where new stars are being born.

Betelgeuse
Pronounced "beetle juice," this brilliant red star marks Orion's shoulder. It is a red supergiant.

Rigel
This blue supergiant, about 775 light-years from Earth, is 70,000 times more luminous than our Sun.

Orion's belt
Look for three bright stars in a row (above). These form the belt across Orion's waist, making the constellation easy to spot.

Horsehead Nebula (NGC 2024)
This pillar of dust (left) looks like a horse's head silhouetted against more distant glowing gas.

Life of a star: Star birth

Stars are born in enormous clouds of gas and dust. Compressed by gravity, these clouds collapse under their own weight and separate into smaller knots of gas, which then grow dense enough to ignite as stars.

Great Orion Nebula
Fierce radiation from newborn stars at the heart of this nebula energizes the gas around it, causing it to glow.

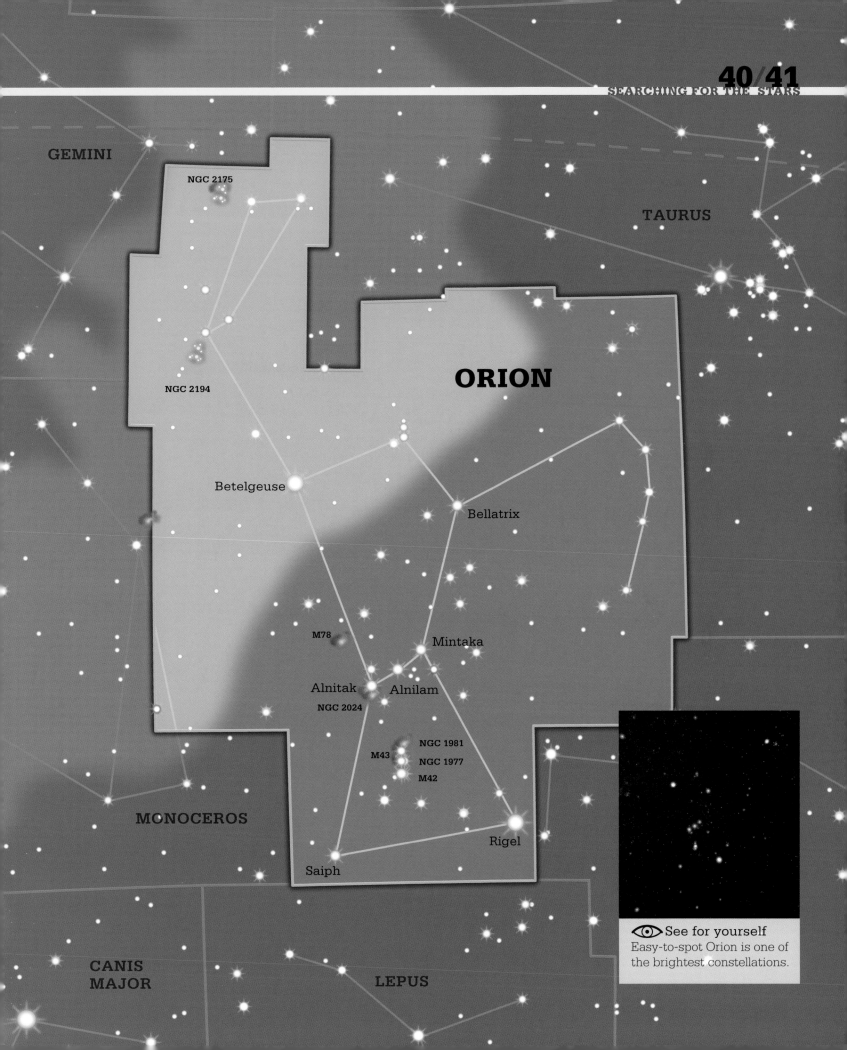

GEMINI

NGC 2175

TAURUS

NGC 2194

ORION

Betelgeuse

Bellatrix

M78

Mintaka

Alnitak   Alnilam

NGC 2024

NGC 1981

M43   NGC 1977

M42

Rigel

MONOCEROS

Saiph

CANIS
MAJOR

LEPUS

👁 See for yourself
Easy-to-spot Orion is one of
the brightest constellations.

Sagittarius [The Archer]

Rich in star clusters and nebulae (gas clouds), this vivid constellation lies in the southern half of the sky. It shines brightly because the middle of the Milky Way lies within its borders.

Origins

For the ancient Greeks, Sagittarius represented a wise centaur named Chiron, an archer with a bow and arrow. A centaur has the torso of a man and the body of a horse.

Taking aim
Sagittarius points his arrow at the heart of the Scorpion (see pages 52–53).

Life of a star: Star clusters

Newborn stars emerge from nebulae in clusters. Those in an open cluster (an irregular group) drift apart over tens of millions of years—we see them only because there are so many short-lived, bright stars. Dense globular (globe-shaped) clusters hold together for much longer.

Globular cluster M22
This ball-shaped cluster in Sagittarius contains many thousands of aging stars.

Sagittarius's highlights

Sagittarius is home to star clouds, nebulae, and dust lanes that hide the center of the Milky Way from view. It is famous for the teapot pattern formed by its eight central stars.

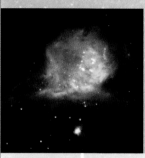

NGC 6822
This small, irregular galaxy, 1.8 million light-years from Earth, contains bright star-forming regions.

Omega/Swan Nebula (M17)
Dense clouds of gas pile up around the edges of this nebula.

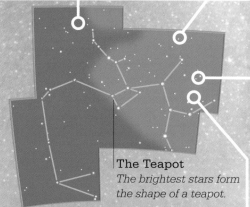

The Teapot
The brightest stars form the shape of a teapot.

Trifid Nebula (M20)
Dark dust lanes separate this famous star-forming nebula into three parts.

Lagoon Nebula (M8)
The Lagoon is one of the brightest nebulae. It is around 4,000 light-years from Earth.

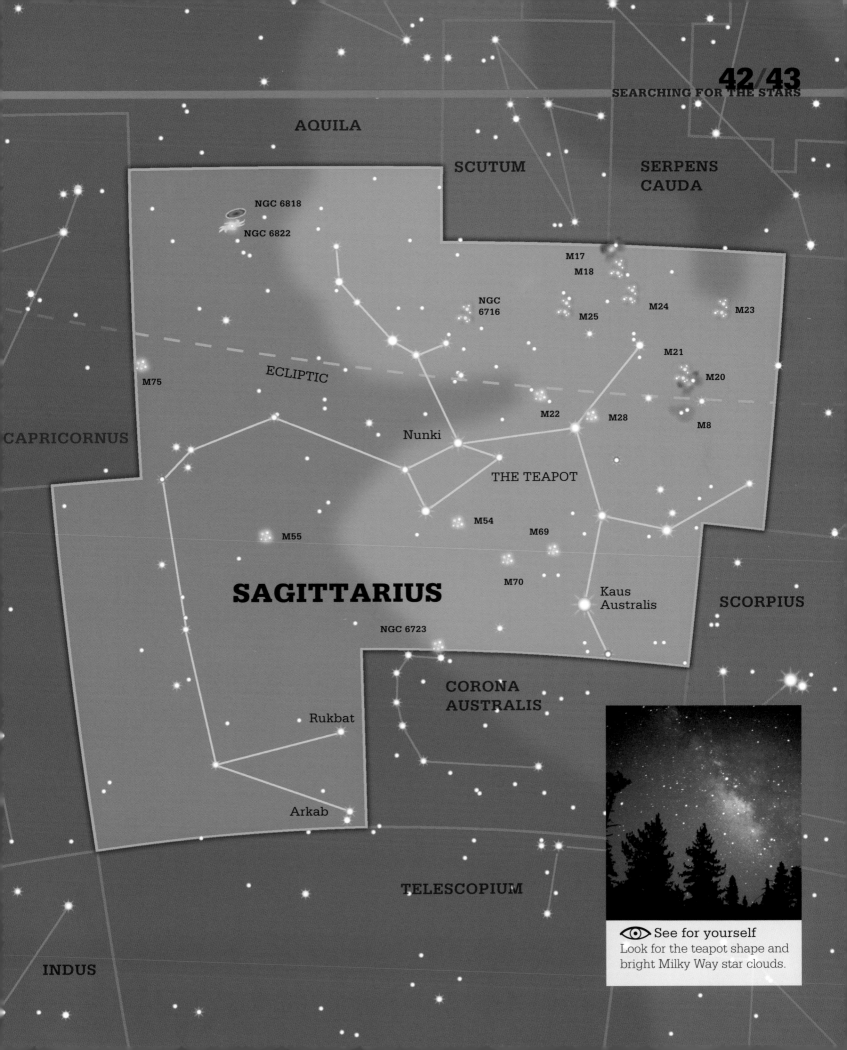

AQUILA

SCUTUM

SERPENS
CAUDA

NGC 6818

NGC 6822

M17

M18

NGC
6716

M25

M24

M23

M21

M20

ECLIPTIC

M75

M22

M28

M8

Nunki

THE TEAPOT

CAPRICORNUS

M54

M55

M69

SAGITTARIUS

M70

Kaus
Australis

SCORPIUS

NGC 6723

CORONA
AUSTRALIS

Rukbat

Arkab

TELESCOPIUM

INDUS

👁 See for yourself
Look for the teapot shape and
bright Milky Way star clouds.

Celestial fireworks

The constellation Carina represents the keel (bottom projection) of a ship from Greek mythology, the *Argo*. It was sailed by the mythical Greek heroes Jason and the Argonauts. Carina lies in the direction of two huge regions of star-forming gas. One is the Carina Nebula (visible to the naked eye), which is around 8,000 light-years away. The other one is an even larger nebula called HD97950, which is 20,000 light-years away.

The star cluster shown at left, embedded in the more distant nebula, is known as NGC3603. Within the cluster is the heaviest star in our galaxy, 116 times the mass of the Sun. Massive stars like this have brief but brilliant lives of just a few million years!

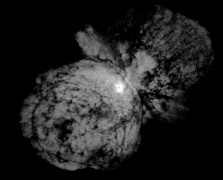

Eta Carinae

Within the Carina Nebula, the star Eta Carinae occasionally erupts violently. It will go on to end its life as a supernova explosion.

Constellation FACT FILE

Common name	The Keel
Abbreviation	Car
Visible from	South of 30° N
Best time to see	January to May, after sunset
Brightest star	Canopus

Southern Hemisphere

Location of Carina

Leo [The Lion]

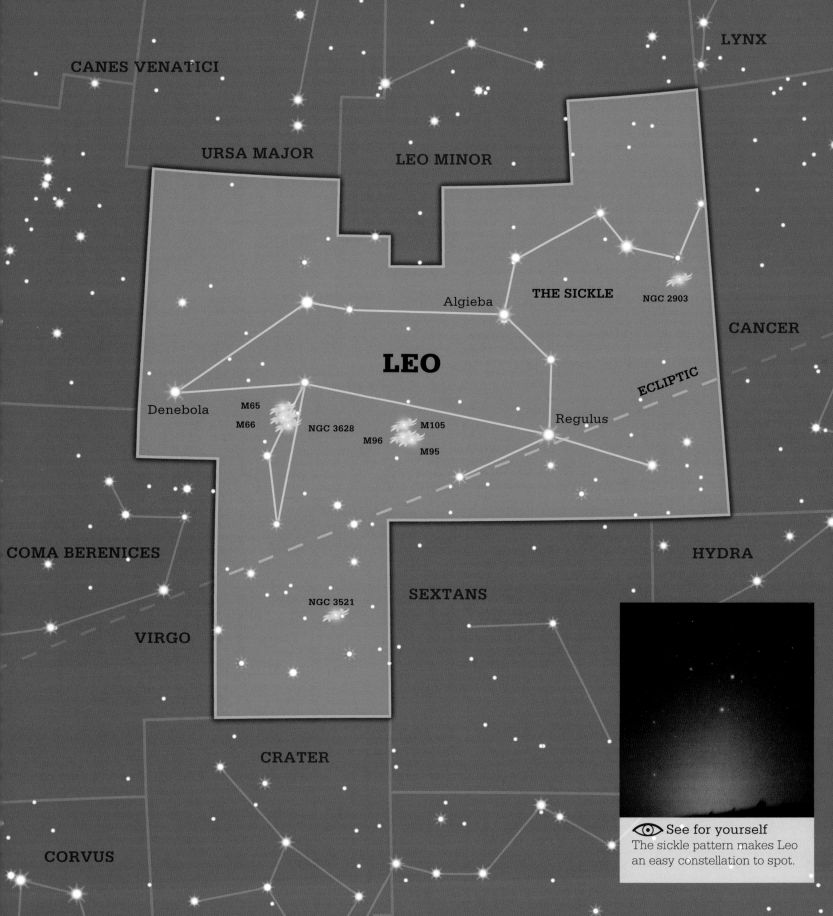

LYNX

CANES VENATICI

URSA MAJOR

LEO MINOR

THE SICKLE

NGC 2903

Algieba

CANCER

LEO

ECLIPTIC

Regulus

Denebola

M65

M66

NGC 3628

M105

M96

M95

COMA BERENICES

HYDRA

SEXTANS

NGC 3521

VIRGO

CRATER

CORVUS

👁 See for yourself
The sickle pattern makes Leo
an easy constellation to spot.

The constellation Leo, located in the Northern Hemisphere, resembles a crouching lion. Lying far from the band of the Milky Way, it is a good place to see distant galaxies.

Constellation FACT FILE

Common name	The Lion
Abbreviation	Leo
Visible from	Worldwide
Best time to see	February to June, after sunset
Brightest star	Regulus

Northern Hemisphere

LOCATION OF LEO

Origins
Leo is usually said to represent the Nemean lion, a ferocious cave monster with an armored hide. The Greek hero Heracles (Hercules to the Romans) had to fight this lion as one of a dozen challenges.

Leo
For thousands of years, the constellation Leo has been viewed as a lion ready to pounce.

Wolf 359
in Leo is one of the closest stars
to Earth but can be seen only **with a large telescope**

Leo's highlights
Most of Leo's brighter stars are in the main sequence of their lives (see box, right), so they show the link between a star's weight and its brightness. For example, the star Regulus is twice as far from Earth as Denebola is, but it appears brighter because it is twice as heavy.

M96 galaxy
This spiral galaxy (above) lies at the heart of a small galaxy group, along with M95 and M105.

M66 galaxy
This spiral galaxy (above) has had its spiral arms distorted and its central nucleus pulled out of place by a close encounter with one of its neighbors.

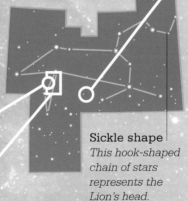

Sickle shape
This hook-shaped chain of stars represents the Lion's head.

Leo triplet
Three spiral galaxies, M65, M66, and NGC 3628 (left), form a small galaxy group near Leo's hind leg. This group is 35 million light-years from Earth.

Life of a star: Main sequence
After an unstable youth, a star spends most of its life shining through hydrogen fusion. In this stage, called the main sequence, the star's brightness depends on its weight (see page 39). The heavier a star is, the hotter and denser its core, and the brighter it shines. Bright stars use their fuel more rapidly and die sooner.

Regulus
The brightest star in Leo is Regulus, 78 light-years from Earth. Lying close to the ecliptic, it is regularly hidden from view from the Earth by the Moon.

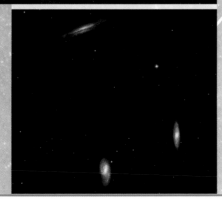

How far? [Big numbers]

The Universe is absolutely enormous, and the spaces between planets, stars, and galaxies are so big that it is impossible for us to visualize them in everyday units of measurement. This is why astronomers use much bigger units of measurement.

The solar system . . . and beyond

Measurements such as miles and kilometers become useless beyond Earth. The distances in interplanetary space are so huge that a good way for us to comprehend them is to reduce space objects to sizes we can understand.

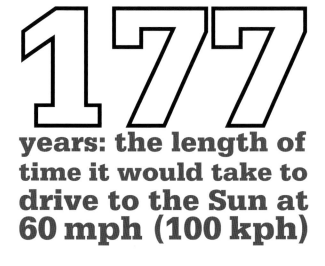

177 years: the length of time it would take to drive to the Sun at 60 mph (100 kph)

Relative distances
By reducing the Earth to the size of a dot and its orbit of the Sun to a small circle, we can better understand its proximity to other space objects.

If this dot represents the size of Earth, then . . .

Moon

. . . the Moon would be 0.5 in. (1.5 cm) away, and . . .

Sun

. . . the Sun would be a ball 21.5 in. (55 cm) across and 19.7 ft. (6 m) away.

If this circle represents the orbit of Earth around the Sun, then . . .

Neptune

Proxima Centauri

. . . Neptune's average orbit would be a circle 6 in. (15 cm) across, and . . .

. . . Proxima Centauri, the nearest star to the Sun, would be 0.4 mi. (0.6 km) away.

Space travel
A spacecraft traveling at 60,000 mph (100,000 kph) would still take 46,000 *years* to reach Proxima Centauri, the closest star to the Sun!

Not so fast!
Science-fiction spacecraft travel much faster than their real-life counterparts.

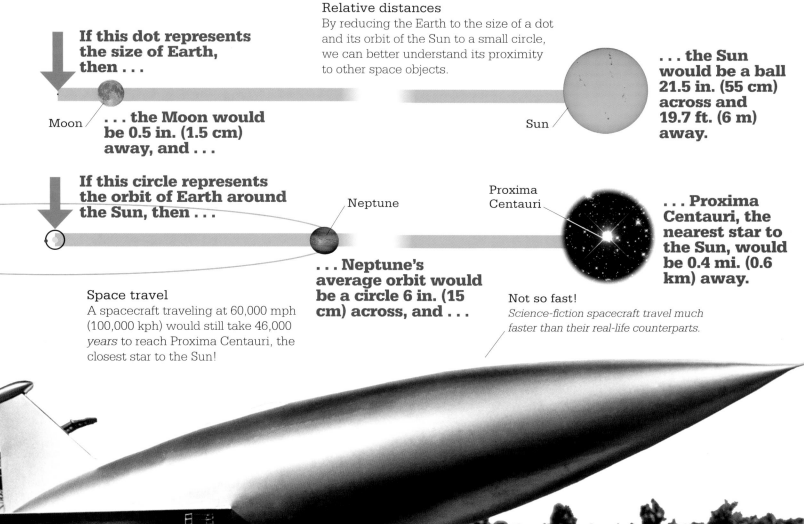

At the speed of light

One way to make sense of the scale of the Universe is to look at how much time light takes to cross huge cosmic distances. Light, the fastest thing in the Universe, moves at 186,000 miles (300,000 km) per second.

Light leaving the Sun takes . . .

8 minutes, 20 seconds . . . to reach **Earth.**

2 hours . . . to reach **Neptune.**

1 year . . . to reach the outer edge of the Oort Cloud, the farthest extent of our solar system.

4.2 years . . . to reach **Proxima Centauri,** the closest star to the Sun.

Light-years
One light-year is the distance that light travels in a year. It is equivalent to 5.9 million million miles (9.5 million million km).

Looking back in time

We see space objects as they were when light left them, so when we look into the Universe, we look back in time. The farther we look, the further back in cosmic time we see. Some galaxies may be so far away, their light hasn't reached Earth yet—perhaps it never will.

Roman times
At 2,000 light-years away, the M25 star cluster in Sagittarius appears to us now as it was during the Roman Empire.

Stonehenge
Light from the Eagle Nebula (M16) began its journey to Earth 5,500 years ago, when Stonehenge was being built in ancient Britain.

Early humans
We see the Andromeda galaxy as it was when the first humans were living, 2.5 million years ago.

Dinosaurs
Light left galaxy NGC 406, in the southern constellation Tucana, 65 million years ago, in the age of the dinosaurs.

Cygnus [The Swan]

Also known as the Northern Cross, Cygnus makes a distinctive pattern against the rich star clouds of the northern Milky Way. It has many fascinating stars and nebulae.

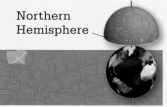

Northern Hemisphere

LOCATION OF CYGNUS

Origins

In Greek myth, Cygnus was the god Zeus in disguise. He changed into a swan to visit a beautiful woman named Leda.

Swan's tail
The star Deneb represents the tail of Cygnus.

Swan's beak
The binary star Albireo marks the tip of the Swan's beak.

Cygnus and Phaeton
In another myth about Cygnus, he was a god transformed into a swan by Zeus to retrieve the body of his friend Phaeton from a river.

Cygnus's highlights

The position of Cygnus against a dense region of the Milky Way makes it a great place to look for unusual objects. These include a famous binary star, a likely black hole (see pages 60–61), and one of the most luminous stars in the sky, Deneb.

Deneb
Cygnus's brightest star is 2,500 light-years from Earth. It is about 160,000 times brighter than the Sun.

Cygnus Rift
A "gap" in the Milky Way shows where dark dust is blocking the light of more distant stars.

North America Nebula (NGC 7000)
Resembling the shape of North America, this nebula is just visible to the naked eye.

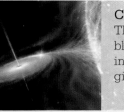

Cygnus X-1
This is a superdense black hole that pulls in nearby matter and gives off X-rays.

Crescent Nebula (NGC 6888)
This glowing bubble (above) was created by gas blowing out from a central star at high speeds.

Veil Nebula (NGC 6992)
The brightest part of the Cygnus Loop, the Veil Nebula is a 60,000-year-old remnant of a supernova (see page 58).

Life of a star: Binaries

Some of the larger knots of gas within star-forming nebulae collapse to form two or more stars. These double (known as binary) or multiple stars usually end up locked in orbit around one another for the rest of their lives.

Albireo
At the southern end of Cygnus, Albireo's yellow and blue components make it one of the most beautiful binaries.

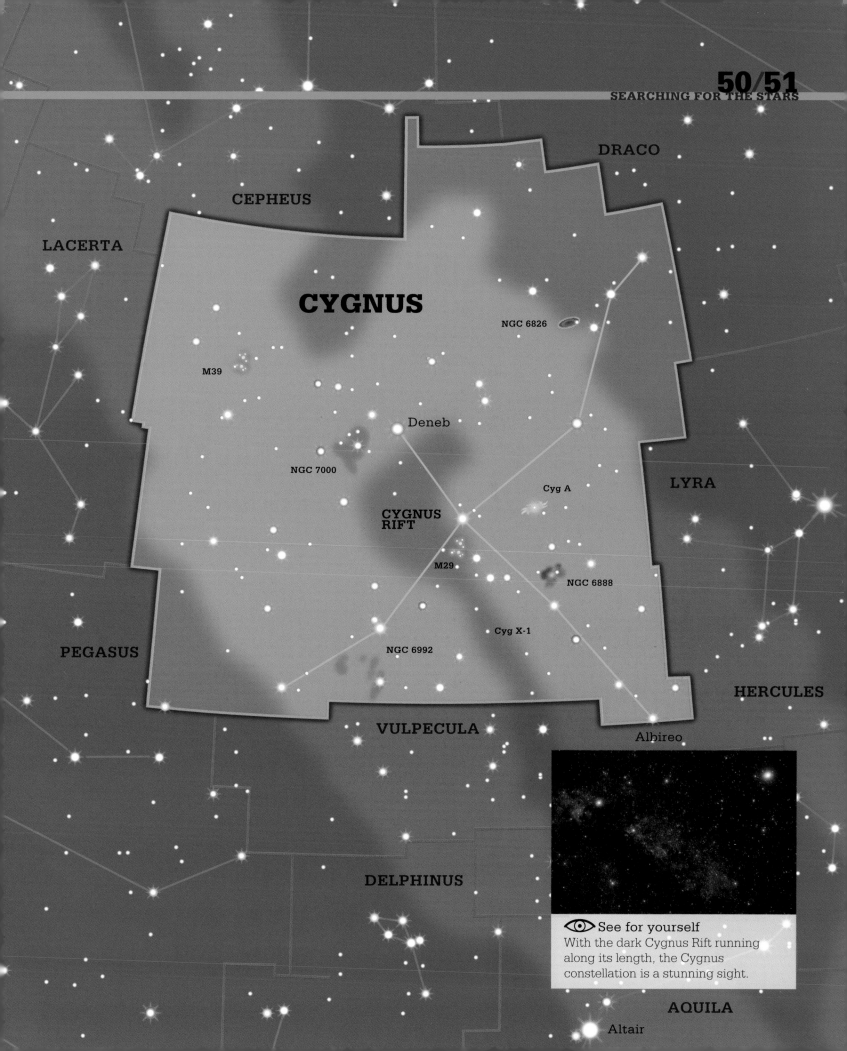

DRACO

CEPHEUS

LACERTA

CYGNUS

NGC 6826

M39

Deneb

NGC 7000

LYRA

Cyg A

CYGNUS RIFT

M29

NGC 6888

Cyg X-1

PEGASUS

NGC 6992

HERCULES

VULPECULA

Albireo

👁 See for yourself
With the dark Cygnus Rift running along its length, the Cygnus constellation is a stunning sight.

DELPHINUS

AQUILA

Altair

Scorpius [The Scorpion]

SERPENS
CAUDA

ECLIPTIC

OPHIUCHUS

Antares

M80

M4

SAGITTARIUS

LIBRA

SCORPIUS

LUPUS

M6

NGC
6383

NGC 6357/
Pismis 24

M7

NGC
6334

Shaula

NGC 6322

NGC
6124

NGC
6231

CORONA
AUSTRALIS

NGC 6388

NGC
6178

NORMA

ARA

See for yourself
Find Scorpius by looking for
Antares and its flanking stars.

Scorpius lies at the southern end of the zodiac, close to the center of the Milky Way. This constellation contains some spectacular stars, nebulae, and star clusters.

Constellation FACT FILE

Common name	The Scorpion
Abbreviation	Sco
Visible from	Worldwide
Best time to see	April to September, after sunset
Brightest star	Antares

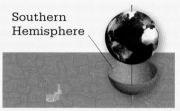

Southern Hemisphere

LOCATION OF SCORPIUS

Origins

In Greek mythology, the hunter Orion (see pages 40–41) was killed by a scorpion's sting. Other myths claim that a scorpion scared Phaeton's flying horses, causing his death (see page 50).

Scorpion
The constellation Scorpius crawls across the Milky Way.

Claws
The stars of Libra once formed the claws of Scorpius but are now their own constellation.

Tail
An arc of stars forms the shape of the Scorpion's tail.

Life of a star: Red giants

When a star runs out of fuel in its core at the end of its life, it keeps on shining by burning hydrogen in shells around the core. This causes it to brighten and swell in size, so its surface cools and it turns orange or red. Depending on its size, it is then called a giant or a supergiant.

Supergiant
Embedded in a glowing cloud of gas, Antares is 65,000 times brighter than the Sun.

Scorpius's highlights

Many of the bright stars in Scorpius are true neighbors in space. They were formed around the same time from the same cloud of star-forming material.

M4 star cluster
A globular cluster (see page 42) lies to the west of Antares.

Stinger
The multiple star Shaula marks the Scorpion's tail.

Betelgeuse
Antares
Our Sun

Antares
A huge star, Antares has a radius of 600 million miles (1 billion km).

Pismis 24 and NGC 6357
This star cluster and associated nebulae contain one of the most massive and luminous stars known.

Cat's Paw Nebula (NGC 6334)
These distinctive blotches are clouds of glowing gas, energized from within by newborn stars that are more than ten times the mass of the Sun.

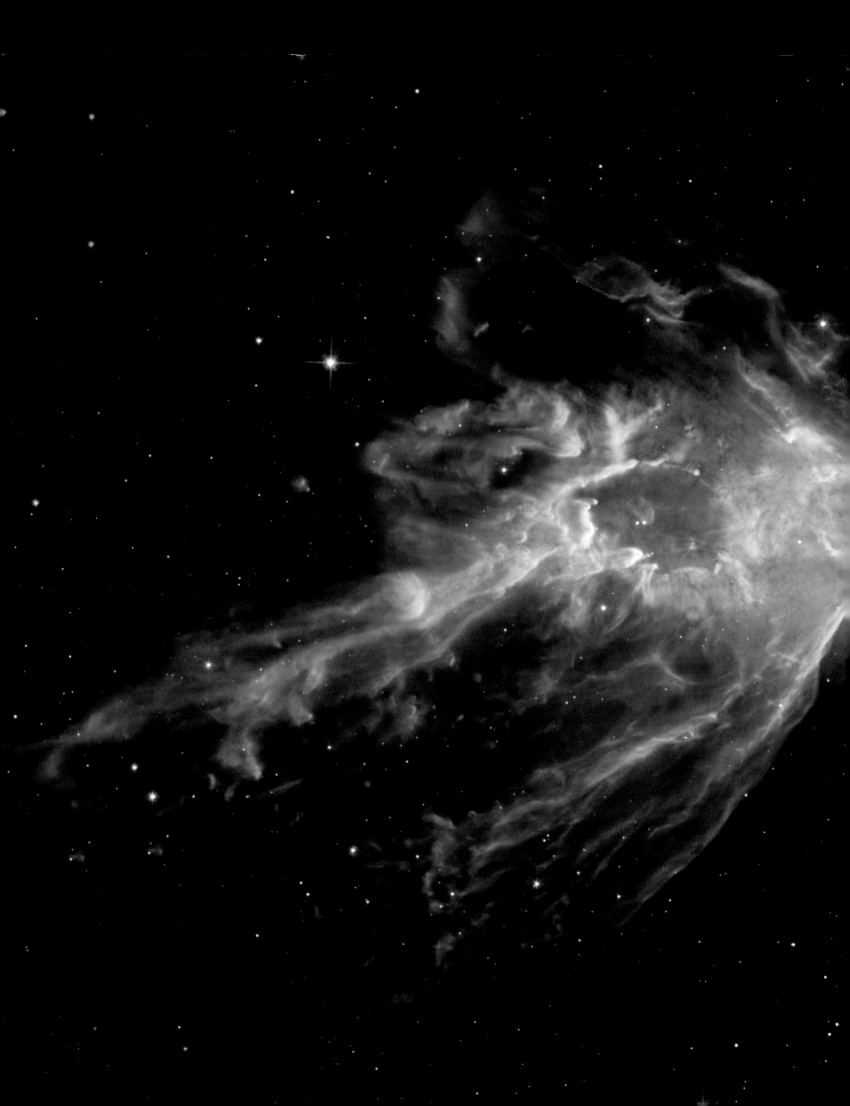

Butterfly emerging

Bubbles of material flung off a dying star have been funneled into an hourglass shape by a ring of dust to form the stunning Butterfly Nebula, in the constellation Scorpius. Behind the dust lies one of the galaxy's hottest stars, burning at 360,000°F (200,000°C).

Lyra [The Lyre]

An ancient musical instrument, the lyre, gives its name to this small constellation in the northern skies. Despite its size, Lyra is packed with magnificent stars and other objects.

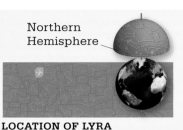

Northern Hemisphere

LOCATION OF LYRA

Origins
In Greek mythology, the lyre—a harplike instrument—was played by the doomed musician Orpheus (far right).

Making music
It was said that when Orpheus played the lyre, it tamed wild animals.

Lost love
Orpheus used music to win back his dead wife, Eurydice, from the Underworld, where the souls of the dead dwelled. But he forgot his promise not to look at her until they were back on Earth, and he lost her again forever.

Lyra's highlights
On the edge of the northern Milky Way, Lyra contains several incredible stars showing different stages in a stellar life cycle.

Bright neighbor
At a distance of just 25 light-years from Earth, Vega is the fifth-brightest star in our skies.

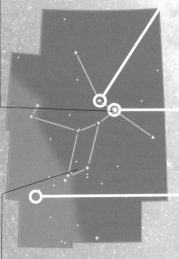

Ring Nebula
This famous planetary nebula lies midway between Lyra's two southernmost stars and can be seen with a small telescope.

Epsilon Lyrae
This amazing quadruple star contains two double stars orbiting each other.

Vega
A bright young star (above), Vega is surrounded by a disk of dusty material that may be forming a new planetary system.

Cluster M56
This star cluster is about 33,000 light-years from Earth.

Life of a star: Dying stars
Eventually, all stars run out of fuel and can no longer keep shining. If a star has roughly the mass of the Sun, it will become an unstable red giant, pulsating and finally flinging off its outer layers in a glowing shell called a planetary nebula. The hot, exhausted core left behind shrinks into a dense white dwarf star (see page 60).

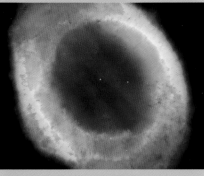

Ring Nebula (M57)
This planetary nebula in Lyra, the remnant of a dying star, forms a ring of gas. Planetary nebulae can look like planets at first glance.

R Lyrae

LYRA

RR Lyrae

CYGNUS

Epsilon Lyrae

Vega

HERCULES

M57

M56

VULPECULA

👁 **See for yourself**
Lyra is easily spotted, thanks
to its bright star Vega.

SAGITTA

Taurus [The Bull]

Instantly recognizable, Taurus (Latin for "bull") looks like the front of a mighty bull charging through the sky toward Orion. It's also home to several intriguing deep-sky objects.

Constellation FACT FILE

Common name	The Bull
Abbreviation	Tau
Visible from	Worldwide
Best time to see	November to February, after sunset
Brightest star	Aldebaran

Northern Hemisphere

LOCATION OF TAURUS

Origins

Taurus is such an obvious bull-like star pattern that it has been recognized since the most ancient times. It may even be depicted in prehistoric cave paintings.

Bull's horn
The star that marks Taurus's upper horn is shared with the neighboring constellation Auriga.

Taurus, the Bull
The distinctive constellation looks like the head and raised front legs of a bull.

Life of a star: Supernovae

As a really massive star grows older, it keeps shining by burning heavier elements. Eventually, though, it collapses under its own weight, triggering a brilliant supernova explosion.

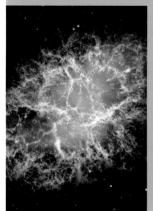

Crab Nebula
These shreds of superhot gas are the expanding remains of a supernova explosion in Taurus, which was seen on Earth in 1054.

Taurus's highlights

Home to two of the most obvious star clusters in Earth's skies, Taurus also contains a supernova remnant from an explosion thousands of years ago.

The Nebra sky disk
The Pleiades, Taurus's famous cluster of stars, can be seen on this sky map from 1600 BCE.

Seven stars
This group of stars is thought to represent the Pleiades.

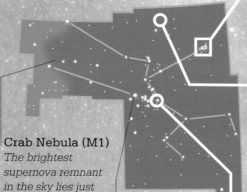

Crab Nebula (M1)
The brightest supernova remnant in the sky lies just above the tip of Taurus's lower horn.

Eye of the bull
Aldebaran marks the Bull's eye.

The Pleiades (M45)
This open cluster (see page 42) of stars is also known as the Seven Sisters because of the number of bright stars it contains.

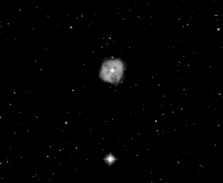

Crystal Ball Nebula (NGC 1514)
This planetary nebula was discovered by astronomer William Herschel in 1790.

The Hyades
This V-shaped star cluster (left) forms the face of the Bull. Taurus's brightest star is Aldebaran.

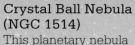

PERSEUS

AURIGA

NGC 1514

Alnath

TAURUS

GEMINI

M45

NGC 1746

PLEIADES

ARIES

M1

NGC 1647

ECLIPTIC

Aldebaran

HYADES

ORION

CETUS

ERIDANUS

👁 See for yourself
The two bright star clusters of the
Hyades and Pleiades make Taurus
an easy constellation to spot.

When a star dies, its remnant, in the form of a superdense burned-out core, collapses. These dead stars can then go on to form some of the strangest objects in the Universe.

Black holes

Very rarely, the weight of a dying star's core is so great that it collapses until all its matter is jammed into a single point. This point seals itself off from the Universe behind a wall called the event horizon. Nothing can escape it.

Spaghettification

If you fell into a black hole, it would pull on your feet more than on your head, stretching you out like spaghetti!

X-rays
Matter falling into the black hole is heated up until it emits high-energy X-rays.

Matter
Objects that get too close to the hole are sucked in.

Warped space
Objects and light passing the hole are deflected from their original courses.

White dwarfs

Once a star like the Sun has blown off its outer layers in a planetary nebula (see page 56), all that is left is the core. This becomes a faint but hot white dwarf, roughly the size of Earth.

Diamond core
A white dwarf is rich in carbon, the same element that, when compressed, forms diamonds.

The hottest known white dwarf has a temperature of 360,000°F

Neutron stars

Stars that weigh as much as eight Suns die in supernova explosions. The forces involved split the stars' atoms and jam the surviving neutron particles together in fast-spinning, very dense neutron stars.

A pinhead's worth of neutron star weighs the same as a supertanker

Event horizon
Nothing, not even light, can escape beyond this point.

Gravity well

Heavyweight star
A neutron star is the densest physical object in the Universe.

The first black hole to be identified was Cygnus X-1, 6,000 light-years away from Earth

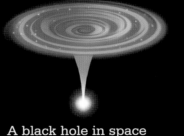

A black hole in space
One way to imagine the effect of a black hole is to think of space as a flat sheet held up and pulled tight, with a deep dent in the middle from a superdense object.

Pulsars
A neutron star (see opposite page) compresses most of a star's original magnetism into a tiny space. This creates a powerful field that channels radiation from the star along two narrow beams. Often, the result is a rapidly flashing pulsar.

- Rotation axis
- Beam of radio waves
- Magnetic pole
- Magnetic field
- Neutron star

Pulsing pulsars
A pulsar is a bit like a cosmic lighthouse. It may flash hundreds of times per second as the star rotates rapidly.

Pulsar flashes
A pulsar only appears "on" when its beam points straight at Earth.

PULSAR OFF   PULSAR ON   PULSAR OFF

More here

A Black Hole Is Not a Hole
by Carolyn Cinami DeCristofano

Scientists in the Field: The Mysterious Universe
by Nic Bishop and Ellen Jackson

black hole
event horizon **pulsar**
spaghettification
Cygnus X-1
white dwarf
neutron star

See for yourself—there's a white dwarf orbiting the brightest star in the sky, Sirius. But the easiest one to see with binoculars is called Eridanus, in the southern hemisphere.

planetary nebula: the gas shell thrown off when a red star dies.

supernova: the blast created when a massive star explodes at the end of its normal life.

X-ray: a form of radiation produced by stars and hot gas clouds.

Discoverin
pla

* Why did people believe there was life on Mars?

* Who took "one small step"?

* What creates a planet's incredible rings?

g amazing

nets

The planets are spherical objects that orbit the Sun. They are often accompanied by moons, which orbit them in turn (see pages 86–87). There are eight planets: four smaller rocky planets in the inner solar system, and four larger gas giants farther from the Sun.

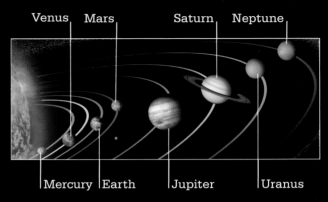

Venus   Mars   Saturn   Neptune

Mercury Earth   Jupiter   Uranus

Rocky planets

Mercury, Venus, Earth, and Mars are all rocky planets. Dominated by solid rock, their surfaces are hard enough to stand on. The rocks inside these planets have separated into layers depending on their weights, producing a core of solid or molten iron and a surface of relatively light rock.

The Sun weighs

743x

more than all the planets put together

Mercury
The smallest of the major planets, Mercury is only slightly larger than Earth's Moon.

Earth
Our home is the largest of the rocky planets. Its molten core powers volcanoes, and it has a dense atmosphere. It is the only planet with oceans.

Venus
The second-largest rocky planet, Venus is just a little smaller than Earth. It is very different from Earth, though, with a dense, toxic atmosphere and searing heat.

Sun
The Sun lies at the center of our solar system and dwarfs the planets. Its powerful gravity keeps them in orbit around it.

Mars
The outermost rocky planet, Mars is about half the size of Earth, with a thin atmosphere and a cold, dry surface.

View from Earth
These images show the other seven planets as seen through a large, high-quality backyard telescope.

MERCURY   VENUS   MARS

Gas giants

Jupiter, Saturn, Uranus, and Neptune are huge compared to the rocky planets. They are mostly deep layers of gas with only small solid cores at their centers.

Jupiter
The biggest planet of all, Jupiter spins so rapidly that it bulges outward at its equator, making it noticeably oval.

Uranus
Uranus is a gigantic ball of gas and liquid. This strange world was the first to be discovered with a telescope.

Saturn
Saturn was the most distant planet known to ancient astronomers, but its famous rings were not discovered until the telescope was invented (see page 18).

Neptune
The most distant major planet, Neptune is a ball of cold, slushy ice. Its outer atmosphere has the fiercest winds in the solar system.

More here

War of the Worlds
by H. G. Wells

Who Is Neil Armstrong?
by Roberta Edwards

KidsAstronomy.com
NASA **gas giants**
rocky planets methane
solar system

Join the NASA Kids' Club
at www.nasa.gov/
audience/forkids/kidsclub/
flash/index.html.

*A Traveler's Guide to
the Planets* (National
Geographic, 2010)

National Air and Space
Museum, The Mall,
Washington, D.C.

Rose Center for Earth and
Space at the American
Museum of Natural
History, 200 Central Park
West, New York, NY

Griffith Observatory,
2800 E Observatory Ave.,
Los Angeles, CA

See for yourself
Distant giants look much smaller than nearby planets because they are so far away.

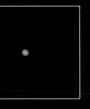

JUPITER

SATURN

URANUS

NEPTUNE

Orbiting the Sun

The huge gravity of our Sun holds planets and other objects—the entire solar system—in orbit around it. The distances in space are so big, they can be measured in astronomical units (AU), equal to the average distance from Earth to the Sun.

Orbiting the Sun
Each orbit follows an oval path that is closer to the Sun at one end than at the other. The orbits of Mercury and Mars are the most irregular paths.

Map of the solar system

The farther a planet is from the Sun, the larger its orbit is and the more slowly the planet will travel around it. The time a planet takes to make a complete orbit of the Sun is its year, while the time it takes to rotate on its axis is its day. The angle at which a planet's poles are tilted creates its seasons.

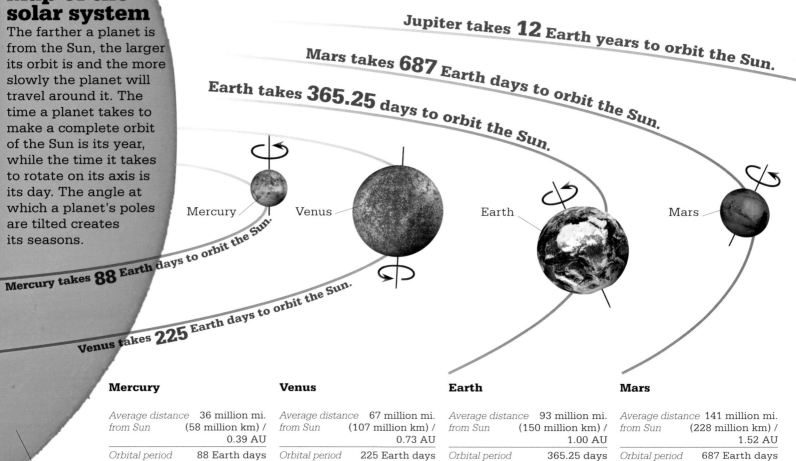

Jupiter takes **12** Earth years to orbit the Sun.

Mars takes **687** Earth days to orbit the Sun.

Earth takes **365.25** days to orbit the Sun.

Mercury takes **88** Earth days to orbit the Sun.

Venus takes **225** Earth days to orbit the Sun.

Mercury

Venus

Earth

Mars

Sun

Mercury

Average distance from Sun	36 million mi. (58 million km) / 0.39 AU
Orbital period	88 Earth days
Tilt of axis	2.1 degrees

Venus

Average distance from Sun	67 million mi. (107 million km) / 0.73 AU
Orbital period	225 Earth days
Tilt of axis	177.3 degrees

Earth

Average distance from Sun	93 million mi. (150 million km) / 1.00 AU
Orbital period	365.25 days
Tilt of axis	23.5 degrees

Mars

Average distance from Sun	141 million mi. (228 million km) / 1.52 AU
Orbital period	687 Earth days
Tilt of axis	25.2 degrees

Planets big and small

The distances and sizes involved in the Universe, and even in our solar system, are so huge that they can be hard to grasp. To get a better idea of the relative sizes of the planets, picture them as these common objects.

SUN = BEACH BALL

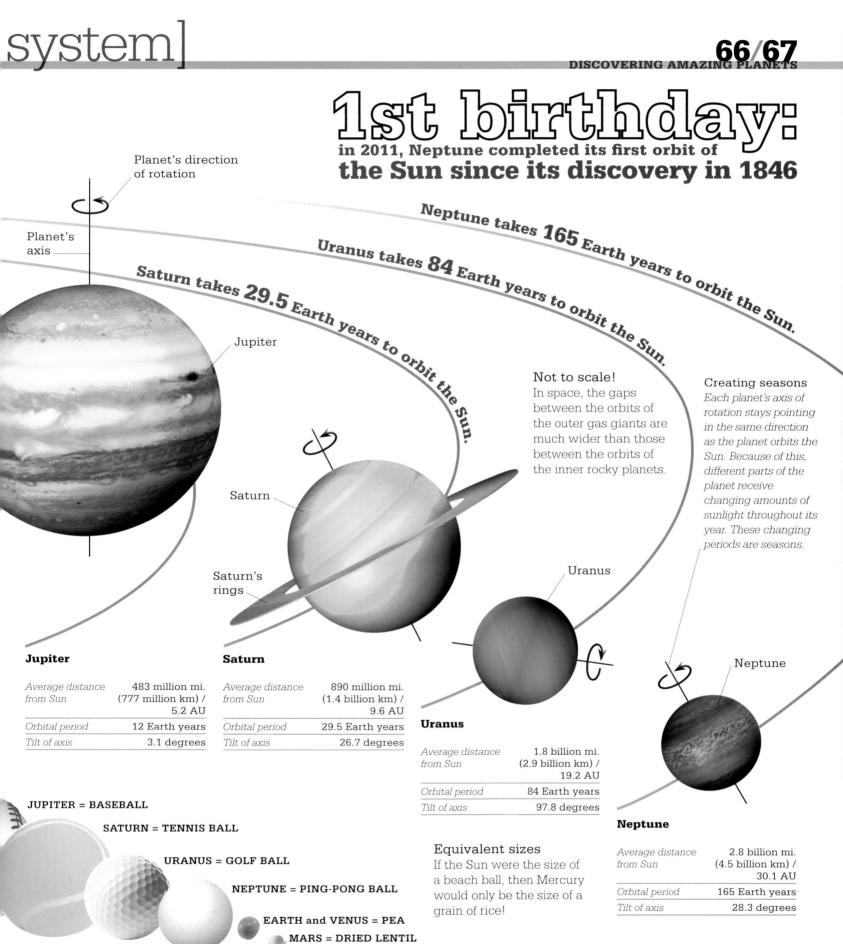

1st birthday:
in 2011, Neptune completed its first orbit of
the Sun since its discovery in 1846

Neptune takes **165** Earth years to orbit the Sun.

Uranus takes **84** Earth years to orbit the Sun.

Saturn takes **29.5** Earth years to orbit the Sun.

Planet's direction of rotation

Planet's axis

Jupiter

Saturn

Saturn's rings

Uranus

Neptune

Not to scale!
In space, the gaps between the orbits of the outer gas giants are much wider than those between the orbits of the inner rocky planets.

Creating seasons
Each planet's axis of rotation stays pointing in the same direction as the planet orbits the Sun. Because of this, different parts of the planet receive changing amounts of sunlight throughout its year. These changing periods are seasons.

Jupiter

Average distance from Sun	483 million mi. (777 million km) / 5.2 AU
Orbital period	12 Earth years
Tilt of axis	3.1 degrees

Saturn

Average distance from Sun	890 million mi. (1.4 billion km) / 9.6 AU
Orbital period	29.5 Earth years
Tilt of axis	26.7 degrees

Uranus

Average distance from Sun	1.8 billion mi. (2.9 billion km) / 19.2 AU
Orbital period	84 Earth years
Tilt of axis	97.8 degrees

Neptune

Average distance from Sun	2.8 billion mi. (4.5 billion km) / 30.1 AU
Orbital period	165 Earth years
Tilt of axis	28.3 degrees

JUPITER = BASEBALL

SATURN = TENNIS BALL

URANUS = GOLF BALL

NEPTUNE = PING-PONG BALL

EARTH and VENUS = PEA

MARS = DRIED LENTIL

MERCURY = GRAIN OF RICE

Equivalent sizes
If the Sun were the size of a beach ball, then Mercury would only be the size of a grain of rice!

The Moon is the most prominent body in the night sky. It revolves around the Earth monthly, reflecting light from the Sun and displaying varying amounts of its surface.

Fixed face

You will only ever see the nearside of the Moon; the far side is never visible from Earth. This is because as the Moon orbits Earth, it also rotates, or spins, on its own axis.

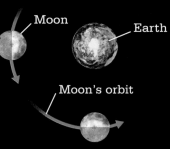

Moon

Earth

Moon's orbit

A nearside view
The Moon orbits Earth and rotates slowly on its axis at exactly the same time. This means that only one face, the nearside, is ever turned toward Earth.

A month of Moon watching

If you observe the Moon regularly for a month, you will see that its shape seems to change. Different parts of the Moon are visible, depending on how much sunlight shines on it. Over a period of 29.5 days, the Moon goes through a cycle of nine phases, from New Moon to Full Moon and back again.

Direction of Moon's orbit

Sun's rays

Moon

Earth's orbit around Sun

Moon's orbit around Earth

Earth

Day 1
At New Moon, only the farside is lit by the Sun.

Day 3
The Sun begins to illuminate part of the nearside.

Day 7
A quarter of the way around the Moon's orbit, half of the nearside is in sunlight.

Day 11
More than half of the nearside is lit. *Gibbous* means "hump shaped."

Monthly cycle
The amount of the Moon's sunlit face we see from Earth changes from day to day over a cycle of 29.5 days. Because the Moon rotates, we only ever see its nearside.

NEW MOON

WAXING CRESCENT

FIRST QUARTER

WAXING GIBBOUS

Earth

Earth's Equator

Moon

Moon's orbit
The Moon's orbit around Earth is tilted at an angle of 5 degrees, relative to Earth's Equator.

Moon's orbit

27.32 days

Eclipses

The Sun and Moon appear exactly the same size in Earth's sky. This means that on rare occasions, when the Earth, Sun, and Moon line up, a solar or lunar eclipse can occur. Do not watch a solar eclipse unless you are wearing special glasses to prevent eye damage.

Solar eclipse
The Moon passes across the face of the Sun. Sunlight is blocked from reaching part of the Earth for a few moments.

Lunar eclipse
The Full Moon passes through Earth's shadow and the Sun's light is blocked out. At the peak of the eclipse, it looks bloodred.

Day 14
The nearside is fully illuminated by the Sun's rays.

Day 17
The sunlight begins to set on the western edge as the Moon wanes, or shrinks.

Day 21
Three-quarters of the way around the Moon's orbit, half of the nearside is lit.

Day 24
By now, only a sliver of sunlight remains on the side of the Moon facing Earth.

Day 29
By day 29, the Moon has returned to the New Moon phase, and the cycle begins again.

FULL MOON

WANING GIBBOUS

LAST QUARTER

WANING CRESCENT

NEW MOON

Moon map

The Moon is our nearest neighbor in space, making it the best subject for detailed observation with the naked eye, binoculars, or a telescope. Like Earth, the Moon has a fascinating and varied landscape.

Best viewing time

Shadows cast by features on the Moon make them easier to see. You can see more details during the first and last quarters (see pages 68–69) than when it's full and the shadows are short.

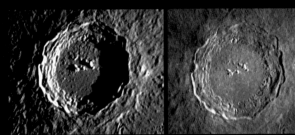

CRATER LIT FROM SIDE   **CRATER LIT OVERHEAD**

Moon shadows

Images taken at different phases show how shadows affect the visibility of the lunar crater Copernicus. Above, it is lit by the Sun from one side (left) and from directly overhead (right).

Near and far sides

We are lucky that the interesting side of the Moon (right), with seas, craters, and mountains, is permanently turned toward Earth. The farside (below) is mostly a wasteland filled with deep craters.

Sea of Moscow

Tsiolkovskiy crater

Nearside
The familiar nearside of the Moon is a mix of dark "seas" (actually rolling plains of ancient solidified lava), and bright, heavily cratered highland regions.

Farside
For still unexplained reasons, the lunar farside has very few dark seas.

Plato crater

BAY OF RAINBOWS

Copernicus crater

SEA OF SHOWERS

OCEAN OF STORMS

Kepler crater

Grimaldi crater

SEA OF CLOUDS

SEA OF MOISTURE

Tycho crater

FROZEN SEA

Lunar Apennine mountains

SEA OF SERENITY

SEA OF CRISES

SEA OF VAPORS

SEA OF FERTILITY

SEA OF NECTAR

"Rays" formed by Tycho impact

Edwin "Buzz" Aldrin
Part of the Apollo 11 mission, Aldrin was the second man to set foot on the Moon.

Exploring the Moon

The Moon has been explored by unmanned space probes since the 1950s. But crossing roughly 250,000 miles (400,000 km) of space to reach the Moon is still an enormous challenge. Only 12 astronauts have so far walked on the Moon, all part of the US Apollo program. The Luna and Lunokhod missions were part of the Soviet program, and Chandrayaan was Indian.

1959 **Luna 2** First crash landing on the Moon

Luna 3 First pictures of the farside of the Moon

1964 **Ranger 7** First close-up photos of the Moon's surface

1966 **Luna 9** First soft landing

Lunar Orbiter 1 First probe in orbit around the Moon

1969 **Apollo 11** First manned Moon landing, by Neil Armstrong and Buzz Aldrin, on July 20

1970 **Lunokhod 1** First robotic lunar rover

1971 **Apollo 15** First use of the Lunar Roving Vehicle

1972 **Apollo 17** Last manned Moon landing—so far!

1976 **Luna 24** First robotic sample return mission

1998 **Lunar Prospector** First detailed mineral mapping of the surface

2008 **Chandrayaan-1** Discovery of water ice on the Moon

"That's one small step for man; one giant leap for mankind"
—Neil Armstrong's first words on the Moon, 1969

Although it is the brightest object in the night sky, at first glance the Moon's landscape may seem dull and gray. But rock samples and close-up views from space probes have revealed a fascinating history and a variety of surface features.

Moon formation

The Moon was formed about 50 million years after the Earth, when a planet the size of Mars smashed into the young Earth. A huge spray of debris was flung into orbit around Earth, where it condensed and solidified into the modern Moon.

Big splash
Astronomers have named the collidi planet Theia, after the mother of the Moon goddess in Greek mythology.

Craters

Nearly all of the craters covering the Moon formed when it was bombarded by meteorites billions of years ago. Many of the craters have terraced walls and central peaks.

TSIOLKOVSKIY CRATER

Seas

Lunar "seas" are dark plains created by lava that flooded the Moon's biggest impact basins up to 3 billion years ago. Solid lava has since been turned to powder by countless tiny impacts.

LUNAR ROVER ON LAVA PLAIN

AITKEN CRATER

COPERNICUS CRATER

EARTH RISING OVER SMYTH'S SEA

Moon rocks

The Apollo missions of the 1960s and 1970s targeted six very different areas of the nearside of the Moon. Astronauts trained as geologists and collected a huge number of Moon rocks. This helped scientists back on Earth build a detailed picture of the Moon's 4.5-billion-year history.

Chipping off
Astronaut Harrison Schmitt collects a rock sample during the Apollo 17 mission.

Valuable finds
This Moon rock was brought back from the Taurus-Littrow region of the Moon by Apollo 17.

842 lb. (382 kg) of Moon rocks have been brought back by astronauts

Mountains

The Moon's mountain peaks were all made by meteorite impacts. They form isolated groups at the centers of large craters, or chains around the edges of the biggest impact basins.

LUNAR APENNINES

Apollo 15 panorama
This spectacular photograph shows the landscape around Hadley Mountain in the Lunar Apennines.

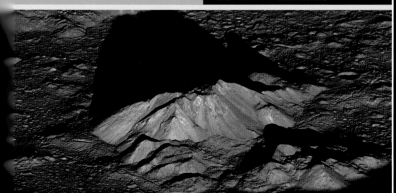

CENTRAL PEAKS OF TYCHO CRATER

Lava tubes

Evidence of small volcanoes like those on Earth is rare on the Moon. But a few winding valleys called lava tubes show where molten rock erupted from cracks and carved its way through the landscape.

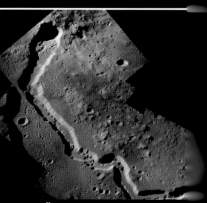

SCHRÖTER'S VALLEY

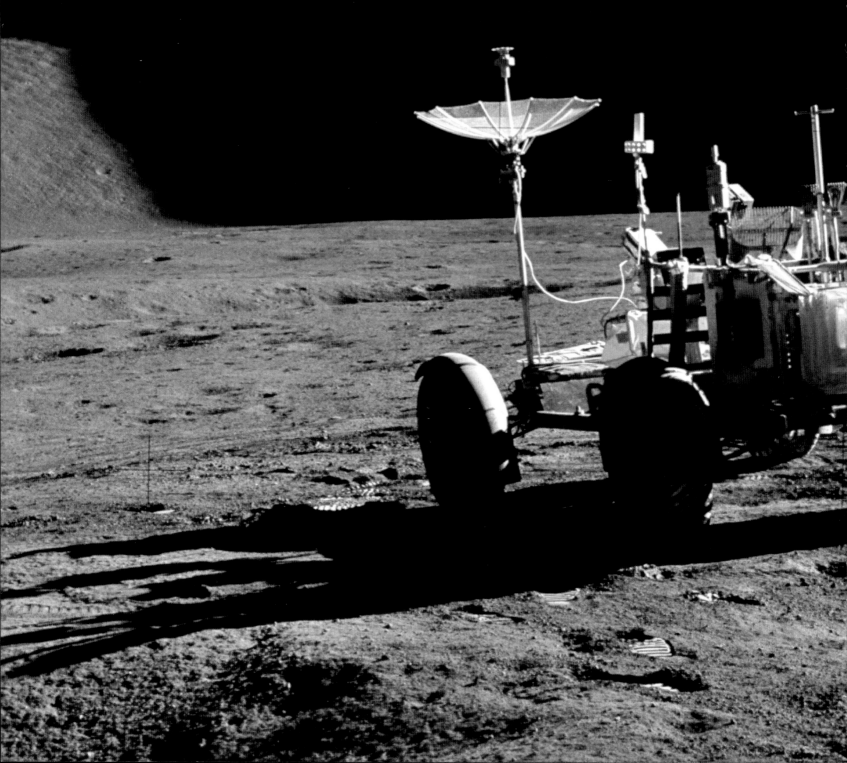

Driving on the Moon

Six Apollo missions landed on the Moon from 1969 to 1972 (see page 71). On the final three missions, a "Moon buggy" (the Lunar Roving Vehicle, or LRV) enabled further exploration of the Moon's surface. Here, James Irwin of Apollo 15 and the LRV are near the foot of Mount Hadley.

Two planets—Mercury and Venus—orbit nearer to the Sun than Earth does (see page 66). For this reason, they are never seen far from the Sun. Mercury is a tiny, fast-moving planet with a scorched, airless surface. Venus is a near twin of Earth in size, cloaked in a dense atmosphere.

WHAT YOU CAN SEE

👁 Eye view | 🔭 Telescope

Viewing notes: Mercury
Mercury can be seen in predawn or sunset skies for just a few days a year, when it is farthest from the Sun. Through a telescope you can see a small disk and perhaps phases.

👁 Eye view | 🔭 Telescope

Viewing notes: Venus
Venus is unmistakable in the morning or evening. If you look through a telescope, Venus's bright cloud tops are revealed, as well as its changing size and shape as it orbits the Sun.

Mercury

It takes less than three months for Mercury to orbit the Sun. It is only visible just before dawn or just after sunset and looks very much like Earth's Moon, with a heavily cratered surface and no air. But it is much hotter—the temperature on Mercury can get hot enough to melt lead. One of Mercury's strangest features is its enormous metal core, which makes up about 40 percent of its interior.

Mercury

Diameter	3,032 miles (4,880 km)—0.38x Earth
Mass (compared to Earth)	0.06x Earth
Gravity (compared to Earth)	0.38x Earth
Rotation period (day)	59 days
Number of moons	0

The surface of Mercury reaches 801°F (427°C)

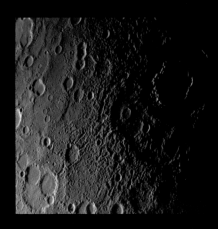

Cratered world
Mercury is dimpled by countless craters from ancient impacts.

MESSENGER to Mercury
Mercury moves so fast that it is very difficult to reach with spacecraft. *MESSENGER*, the first probe to study Mercury in detail, took seven years to enter its orbit, finally arriving in 2011.

Water on Mercury?
While temperatures soar in daylight, Mercury is a freezing –290°F (–180°C) at night. Deep impact craters near Mercury's poles never get sunlight at all. Astronomers think they might be filled with ice left behind by collisions with comets.

Venus

The closest planet to Earth, Venus shines brilliantly in the morning or evening sky. As Venus orbits the Sun, we see different amounts of its sunlit side, giving Venus phases just like those of Earth's Moon (see pages 68–69). The phases can be seen through a small telescope.

Brightest light
Venus is the third-brightest object in our sky, after the Sun and Moon.

Venus

Diameter	7,520 miles (12,102 km)— 0.95x Earth
Mass (compared to Earth)	0.82x Earth
Gravity (compared to Earth)	0.91x Earth
Rotation period (day)	243 days
Number of moons	0

Choking atmosphere
Venus's atmosphere is far denser than Earth's, and dominated by toxic carbon dioxide. It heats the planet to around 860°F (460°C) and exerts crushing pressures.

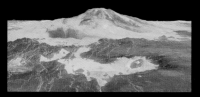

Beneath the clouds
Space probes can fire radar beams into Venus's atmosphere to map its surface.

Landing on Venus
From the 1960s–1980s, a series of Russian *Venera* space probes tried to land on Venus. The first melted before they reached the surface, but with heavy shielding, later missions, such as Venera 14, sent back pictures for a few minutes.

Volcanic world
Radar maps of Venus reveal a planet shaped by volcanic eruptions.

Mars [The red one]

Famous for its red color, Mars is one of the most visible planets. Despite having a cold, dry surface, it is the most Earth-like of the rocky planets, with huge amounts of hidden water.

Surface of Mars

Mars's landscape is a mixture of heavily cratered highlands and lowland plains. It is covered in evidence of past natural activity, from huge volcanoes to floodplains and river valleys. Mars's poles even have bright ice caps similar to those on Earth.

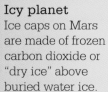

Mars rovers
NASA has sent wheeled robots to Mars to investigate this fascinating planet.

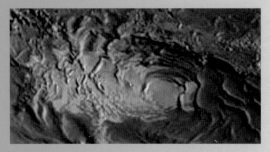

Icy planet
Ice caps on Mars are made of frozen carbon dioxide or "dry ice" above buried water ice.

River valley
Mars has steep-sided valleys carved by flowing water. This is evidence that the planet was once warmer and wetter than it is today.

Mars looks red-hot but is in **fact very** C O L D

Olympus Mons

Tharsis volcano chain

Mars

Diameter	4,222 miles (6,795 km)—0.53x Earth
Mass (compared to Earth)	0.107x Earth
Gravity (compared to Earth)	0.38x Earth
Rotation period (day)	24 hours, 39 minutes
Number of moons	2

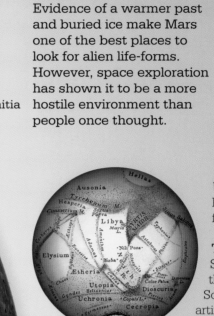

North pole

Acidalia Planitia

Chryse Planitia

Kasei Valles

Lunae Planum

Eos Chasma

Valles Marineris

South pole

Life on Mars?

Evidence of a warmer past and buried ice make Mars one of the best places to look for alien life-forms. However, space exploration has shown it to be a more hostile environment than people once thought.

War of the Worlds

H. G. Wells's 1898 novel was the first story of a Martian invasion.

The watery planet

Some scientists thought that this map of Mars, by Giovanni Schiaparelli in the 1870s, showed artificial waterways. The "canals" he observed turned out to be an illusion.

World of extremes

Mars's terrain is hugely varied, from the highest volcanoes in the solar system to the deepest canyons. The red planet's unique color comes from iron oxide minerals found in its rocks.

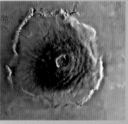
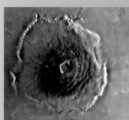

Olympus Mons

Molten rock has oozed onto the surface, creating the biggest volcano in the solar system.

Olympus Mons
*86,614 ft.
(26,400 m) high*

Mount Everest on Earth
29,016 ft. (8,844 m) high

Grand Canyon on Earth
*1.6 mi. (2.5 km) deep, 29 mi.
(47 km) wide*

Valles Marineris
*6–9 mi. (10–14 km)
deep, 250 mi.
(400 km) wide*

Vast landscape

In places, Mars's surface has collapsed under its own weight to create deep cracks and canyons, such as Valles Marineris. The largest Martian volcano is Olympus Mons.

Jupiter [The giant]

Jupiter, the biggest planet in the solar system, could contain all the others with room to spare. It is a giant ball of gas surrounded by bands of light and dark clouds, with fierce storms that can grow larger than the entire Earth.

Jupiter

Diameter	88,846 miles (142,984 km)—11.21x Earth
Mass (compared to Earth)	318x Earth
Gravity (compared to Earth)	2.53x Earth
Rotation period (day)	9 hours, 56 minutes
Number of moons	63

Red spots

Jupiter's most obvious feature is a red oval known as the Great Red Spot (GRS), which is an atmospheric storm twice the size of Earth. The GRS has been visible to astronomers for at least 200 years; it is sometimes accompanied by other, smaller spots.

Getting up close
This color picture of Jupiter was taken by the *Cassini* space probe in 2000.

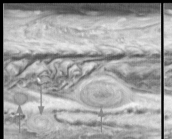 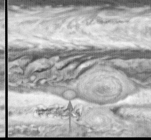 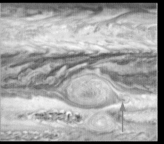

May 15, 2008
Three red spots circle Jupiter in its southern hemisphere.

June 28, 2008
The smallest spot begins to collide with the Great Red Spot.

July 8, 2008
The smallest spot is absorbed completely by the giant storm.

Gas giant

Jupiter's gaseous content makes it more like the Sun than any other planet is. It will never be possible to land on Jupiter. The bands, swirls, and spots on its surface are all a result of its cloudy atmosphere.

Liquid hydrogen interior

Outer atmosphere

Core

Metallic hydrogen

Inside Jupiter
Jupiter's core is probably solid, but it is surrounded by gaseous material, mainly hydrogen.

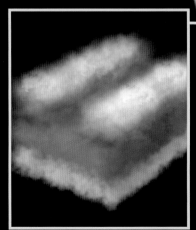

Jupiter's surface
It is the bright yellow and red clouds swirling around Jupiter that give it such a striking, colorful appearance.

Cloud belt

Great Red Spot

CALLISTO

GANYMEDE

EUROPA

IO

moons

Jupiter's moons

Jupiter has a huge family of 63 known moons, 4 of which are roughly the size of Earth's Moon. These 4 moons (at left) were discovered by Italian astronomer Galileo in 1609. They are known as the Galilean moons.

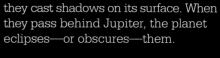

Io casts a shadow

When moons pass in front of Jupiter, they cast shadows on its surface. When they pass behind Jupiter, the planet eclipses—or obscures—them.

Comet catcher

Jupiter's vast size and gravity cause comets and asteroids to crash-land into it. These huge explosions leave long-lasting dark "scars" in Jupiter's clouds.

Comet killer

In 1994, Jupiter pulled the comet Shoemaker-Levy 9 to its doom. This caused the largest explosion ever seen in the solar system.

1,321:
the number of Earths Jupiter could swallow

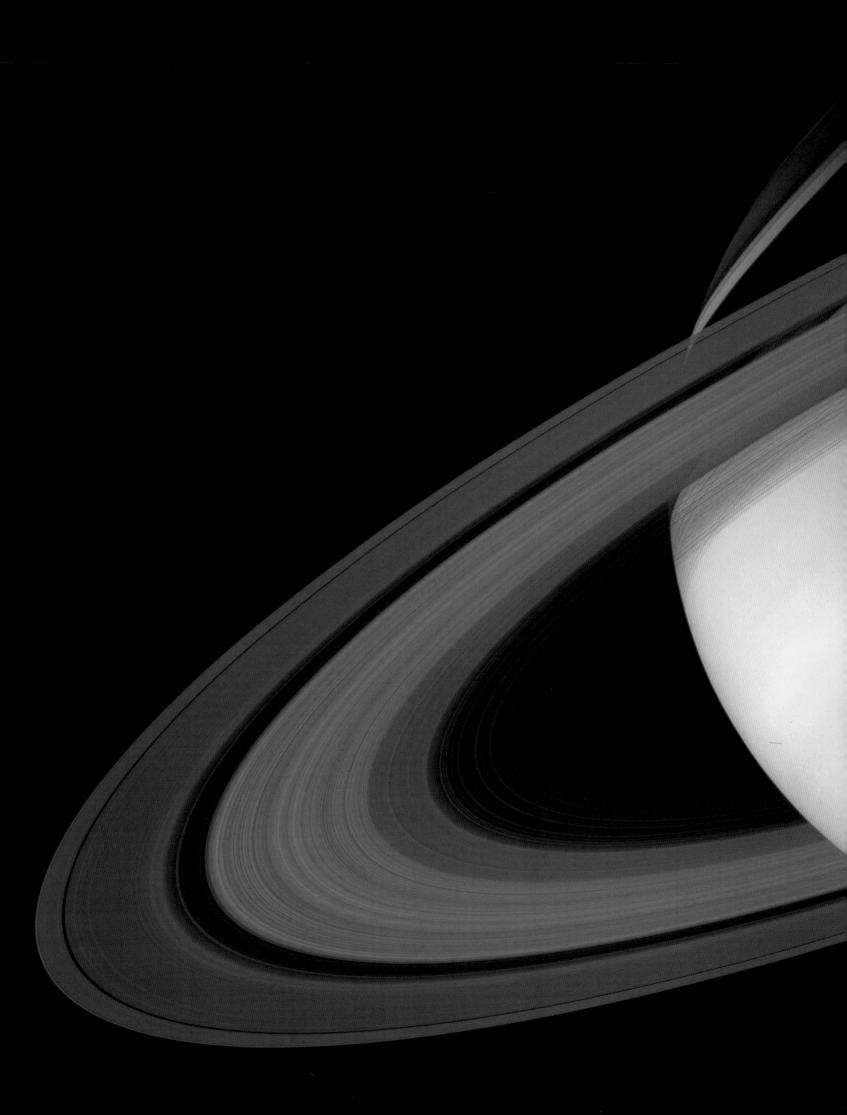

Saturn's rings

Saturn, the most distant planet visible to the naked eye, is best known for its spectacular rings. All the giant planets have ring systems made up of fragments of rock and ice, but Saturn's rings are the most impressive, with a diameter of 174,000 miles (280,000 km). The image, left, was taken by NASA's *Cassini* space probe in orbit around Saturn. It shows both the rings and the deep shadows they cast on Saturn's surface.

OCTOBER 1996

OCTOBER 1997

OCTOBER 1998

NOVEMBER 1999

NOVEMBER 2000

Changing view

Saturn's axis is tilted at 26 degrees, so we see it from different angles as it orbits the Sun. This affects how the rings appear to us.

Outer planets [Icy]

The solar system's outermost planets, Uranus and Neptune, are sometimes called the ice giants, because below their surfaces are layers of water and ice. Beyond Neptune lies the Kuiper Belt, a cloud of small ice dwarfs, including Pluto.

Uranus

Uranus, the first planet to be discovered with a telescope, was spotted in 1781 by astronomer William Herschel, using a telescope he built himself in his backyard in Bath, England. In fact, Uranus is just about bright enough to see with the naked eye, if you know where to look.

Herschel's telescopes
German-born astronomer William Herschel built over 400 telescopes.

Placid world
The *Voyager 2* space probe flew past Uranus for the first time in 1986. It revealed an apparently featureless planet about half the size of Saturn, with a pale blue atmosphere.

Uranus

Diameter	31,763 miles (51,118 km)— 4.01x Earth
Mass (compared to Earth)	14.5x Earth
Gravity (compared to Earth)	0.89x Earth
Rotation period (day)	17 hours, 14 minutes
Number of moons	27

WHAT YOU CAN SEE

Viewing notes
It is possible to spot Uranus using binoculars, but you will see more if you look through a telescope. It looks like a blue-green disk.

🔭 Telescope

Rings
Uranus is surrounded by a system of 13 narrow rings.

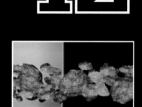

Dark rings
Uranus has dark rings that are composed of large chunks of frozen methane.

Colorful planet
Methane in Uranus's atmosphere absorbs red light, so the planet appears to be a blue-green color.

Winter at north pole

Summer at south pole

Spring/fall

Sun

Summer at north pole

Spring/fall

Winter at south pole

Strange seasons
Uranus's extreme tilt causes a particular pole to point to the Sun for many years, causing strange seasons. Each pole has 42 years of daylight followed by 42 years of night.

Bright clouds
The highest clouds on Uranus appear white. The lowest clouds appear dark blue.

Changing weather
Observations from Earth have shown that Uranus is far stormier now than it was in the 1980s, and that it has bright clouds. Its weather changes with its long seasons.

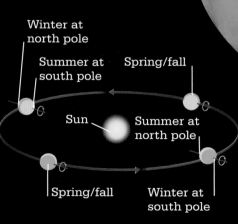

Neptune

Discovered in 1846, Neptune is slightly smaller than Uranus and a slightly deeper blue. It is a much more active world, with the highest winds in the solar system and dark storms raging in its atmosphere.

Neptune

Diameter	30,755 miles (49,495 km)— 3.89x Earth
Mass (compared to Earth)	17.1x Earth
Gravity (compared to Earth)	1.14x Earth
Rotation period (day)	16 hours, 7 minutes
Number of moons	13

Clouds over Neptune
Streams of bright clouds stretc around Neptune at high altitud casting their shadows onto the deeper blue atmosphere below.

Great Dark Spot
Voyager 2 discovered a huge storm on Neptune in 1989, but it seems these big storms last only a few years.

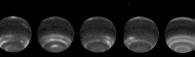

CHANGING WEATHER ON NEPTUN

WHAT YOU CAN SEE

Viewing notes
If you can find Uranus, you can usually find Neptune, too. It is best spotted with a small telescope, using a locator chart. It appears faint and bluish.

✴ Telescope

1,367 mph (2,200 kph): the speed of storm winds on Neptune

Pluto

Tiny Pluto was discovered in 1930 after a deliberate search and was classified as a planet until 2006. Although we now know that it is just one of many ice dwarfs, its icy surface and thin atmosphere are still fascinating. It isn't possible to see Pluto through even a large backyard telescope, because it blends in among countless faint stars.

Pluto and its moons

Charon, Pluto's largest moon, is half the size of its parent planet, and the two keep the same faces permanently turned toward each other. Pluto has at least three other small moons.

Pluto

Diameter	1,442 miles (2,322 km)— 0.18x Earth
Mass (compared to Earth)	0.002x Earth
Gravity (compared to Earth)	0.07x Earth
Rotation period (day)	6 days, 9 hours
Number of moons	4

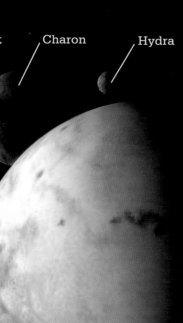

Charon

Hydra

Pluto

The Kuiper Belt

Around and beyond the orbit of Neptur lie countless smaller icy worlds, in a doughnut-shaped ring called the Kuipe Belt. These ice dwarfs range from smal rocks to worlds larger than Pluto—such as Eris, discovered in 2005.

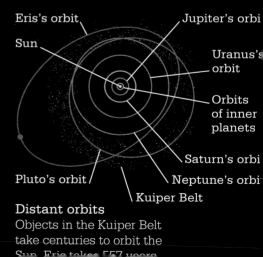

Eris's orbit

Sun

Jupiter's orbi

Uranus's orbit

Orbits of inner planets

Saturn's orbi

Neptune's orbi

Pluto's orbit

Kuiper Belt

Distant orbits
Objects in the Kuiper Belt take centuries to orbit the

Moons [Of the solar system]

Earth isn't the only planet that has a moon. Five other planets have families of moons, ranging from tiny captured asteroids to complex worlds that can be as large as planets themselves.

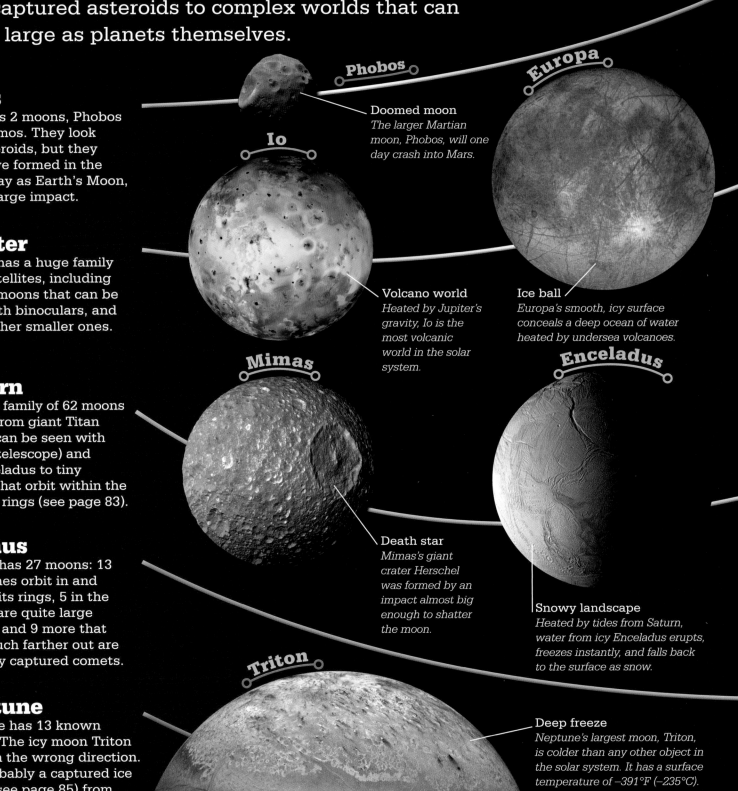

Mars

Mars has 2 moons, Phobos and Deimos. They look like asteroids, but they may have formed in the same way as Earth's Moon, after a large impact.

Jupiter

Jupiter has a huge family of 63 satellites, including 4 giant moons that can be seen with binoculars, and many other smaller ones.

Saturn

Saturn's family of 62 moons ranges from giant Titan (which can be seen with a small telescope) and icy Enceladus to tiny worlds that orbit within the planet's rings (see page 83).

Uranus

Uranus has 27 moons: 13 small ones orbit in and around its rings, 5 in the middle are quite large and icy, and 9 more that orbit much farther out are probably captured comets.

Neptune

Neptune has 13 known moons. The icy moon Triton orbits in the wrong direction. It is probably a captured ice dwarf (see page 85) from the Kuiper Belt.

Phobos

Doomed moon
The larger Martian moon, Phobos, will one day crash into Mars.

Io

Volcano world
Heated by Jupiter's gravity, Io is the most volcanic world in the solar system.

Europa

Ice ball
Europa's smooth, icy surface conceals a deep ocean of water heated by undersea volcanoes.

Mimas

Death star
Mimas's giant crater Herschel was formed by an impact almost big enough to shatter the moon.

Enceladus

Snowy landscape
Heated by tides from Saturn, water from icy Enceladus erupts, freezes instantly, and falls back to the surface as snow.

Triton

Deep freeze
Neptune's largest moon, Triton, is colder than any other object in the solar system. It has a surface temperature of −391°F (−235°C).

Ganymede

Callisto

Hyperion

Titan

Miranda

Crater world
Inactive compared to Jupiter's other giant moons, Callisto is the most heavily cratered world in the solar system.

Jumbled surface
Ganymede has a complex surface that has evolved over time.

Shattered remnant
Spongy-looking Hyperion began as the core of a larger moon that was smashed apart by a giant impact.

Complex world
Titan is the only moon with an atmosphere, beneath which lies an Earth-like surface with lakes of liquid chemicals.

Frankenstein moon
Miranda's mixed-up landscape is so weird that astronomers think it was almost torn apart by tidal forces before reassembling itself.

Jupiter's moon

Ganymede is the
biggest of all: its diameter is
3,268 miles (5,260 km)

Flying objects

In addition to the planets and their moons, smaller objects in our solar system also orbit the Sun. These range from small, rocky asteroids in the warm inner region of the solar system, to icy comets that spend most of their time on the cold edges, although they occasionally come closer to the Sun and warm up.

COMET

SUN

ASTEROIDS

Asteroid belt

Most asteroids are found in the asteroid belt, which is a region between the orbits of Mars and Jupiter. The largest known asteroid is Ceres, which has a diameter of 590 miles (950 km). Asteroids are debris left over from the solar system's formation; Jupiter's powerful gravity prevented them from consolidating into a planet.

MARS

Comets

Most comets orbit beyond Neptune, in the Kuiper Belt (see page 85) or even farther out in a region called the Oort Cloud. Occasionally—when they are disturbed— they fall toward the Sun, which melts the ice inside them and causes them to develop extended halos and tails.

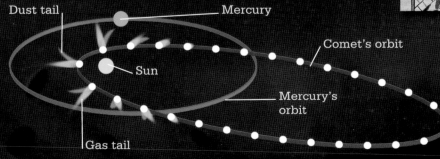

Dust tail

Mercury

Comet's orbit

Sun

Mercury's orbit

Gas tail

Halley's Comet

Halley's Comet passes the Sun every 76 years. Its appearance in 1066 was sewn into the Bayeux Tapestry, a French historical record.

Comet's tail

Solar wind (see page 36) always blows a comet's tail away from the Sun. Comets often have two tails, one made of gas and one of dust.

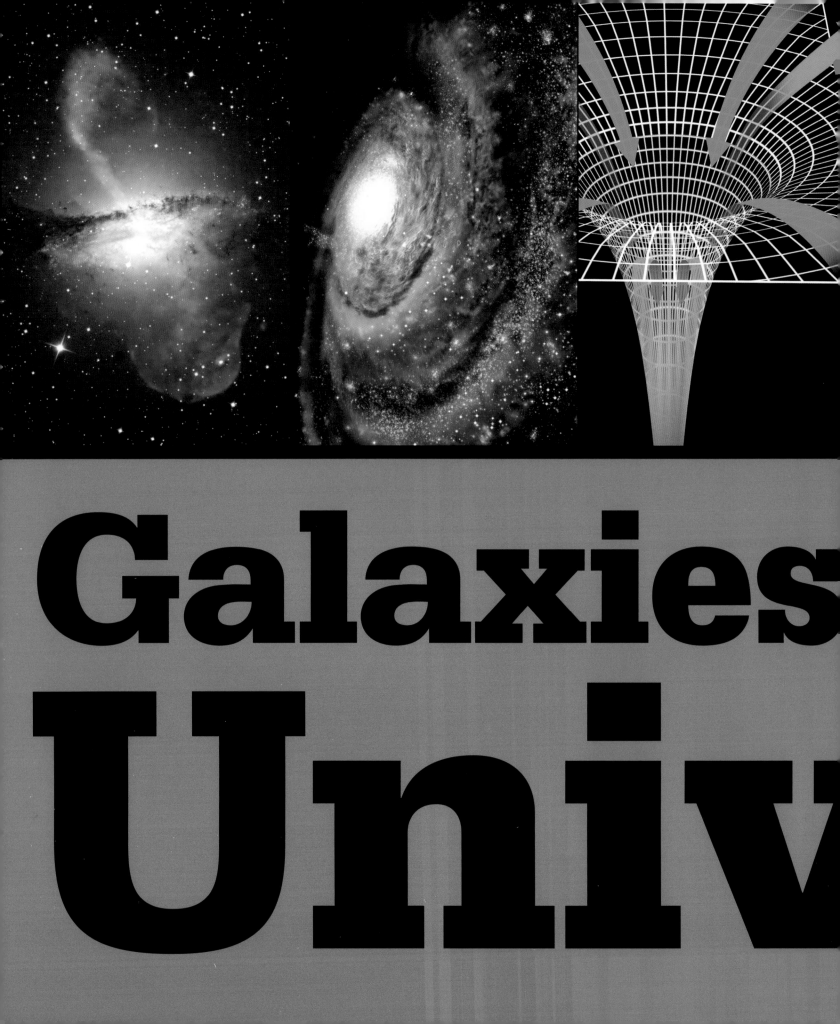

Galaxies
Univ

* How old is the Universe?

* What's on course to collide with the Milky Way?

* Can anything escape a black hole?

and the

erse

Our galaxy [The Milky Way]

All the stars we can see in the sky are just a tiny fraction of those in our galaxy, the Milky Way. This enormous spiral galaxy is home to our Sun and its solar system, including Earth.

You are here

By measuring the distance and distribution of stars around the Milky Way, astronomers know that our Sun is an insignificant star. It lies near a spiral arm 26,000 light-years (see page 49) from the center of the Milky Way, roughly halfway across a broad disk that is 100,000 light-years across.

Our solar system
The Sun and its planets are located about halfway between the center and an edge of the galaxy.

Milky Way galaxy
This illustration shows the Milky Way, looking toward the packed stars of the central bulge.

400,000,000,000:

Band across the sky
This panoramic photograph shows the entire Milky Way wrapping around the sky, as seen from Earth. The brightest star clouds and nebulae lie toward the middle of our galaxy.

Shapes in space

Different stars dominate various parts of the Milky Way. Old red and yellow stars are packed in the central bulge, while newer ones circle in a flattened disk. Hot blue and white stars are concentrated in the spiral arms.

Spiral arms
The arms are not fixed structures—they are concentrations of bright stars.

OVERHEAD VIEW

Oval shape
From the side, the Milky Way looks like a pair of back-to-back fried eggs.

SIDE VIEW

Central bulge
Yellow and red stars orbit in an oval clump.

The Carina Nebula
Newborn stars emerge along the spiral arms. The brightest stars live and die before they can ever move out of the arms.

Our view

When we look in some directions from Earth, we see across the Milky Way, so we see lots of stars behind one another, forming dense star clouds. In other directions, we are looking beyond the Milky Way and so see fewer stars.

Viewing up
Look past the stars of the Milky Way and you will see the space betweeen our galaxy and others.

Earth

Looking out from Earth
As we look in different directions, we see very different views of the Milky Way.

Viewing across
Countless stars form a bright, cloudlike band across the sky.

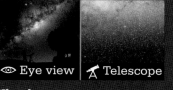

WHAT YOU CAN SEE

◉ Eye view   ⚲ Telescope

Viewing notes
From a dark location, you can see the pale band of the Milky Way, striped by dark rifts of light-absorbing dust clouds that lie in front of it. If you look through binoculars or a telescope, you will be able to see that the band is made up of countless separate stars.

the number of stars in the Milky Way

Dark heart

The core of the Milky Way, 26,000 light-years from Earth, is held together by an enormous black hole (see pages 60–61), which has the mass of several million Suns. Stars in the central bulge orbit the black hole and stay out of its reach, but it still gives off radio waves as gas drifts into its grasp and heats up.

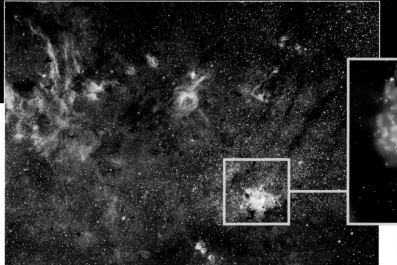

An infrared view of the galaxy
Dense star clouds prevent us from seeing all the way inside our galaxy in visible light, but infrared views can reveal hidden features, such as these dust clouds.

Center of the Milky Way
This X-ray view shows the very heart of our galaxy. We can see the hot gas clouds surrounding the central black hole, known as Sagittarius A* (pronounced "A-star").

The Milky Way

On a dark, moonless night on Réunion
Island in the Indian Ocean, Earth's galaxy,
the Milky Way, extends a spectacular band
across the sky. Brilliant blues and whites
indicate the brightest young star clusters.
The pinkish patches are nebulae (see page

Cloud galaxies [Neighbors]

The Milky Way is so huge that its gravity pulls smaller galaxies into orbit around it. The largest of these are irregular galaxies called the Large and Small Magellanic Clouds.

Magellan's galaxies

The clouds were known to people in the Southern Hemisphere for thousands of years. The first European to record them was Portuguese navigator Ferdinand Magellan, on an around-the-world voyage in 1519–22.

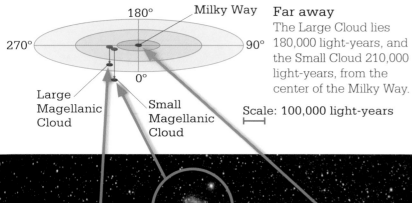

Far away
The Large Cloud lies 180,000 light-years, and the Small Cloud 210,000 light-years, from the center of the Milky Way.

Scale: 100,000 light-years

Large Magellanic Cloud (LMC)

The Large Cloud is both closer to Earth and measurably larger than the other cloud, at about 14,000 light-years across. It is rich in gas, dust, star-forming regions, and newborn heavyweight stars. Many of its stars are lined up along a central bar, and it may have just a single spiral arm.

NGC 2074 star cluster
Formation of this cluster may have been triggered by the shock wave from a supernova (see page 58).

Supernova 1987A
A glowing ring marks the remains of a star that exploded in 1987.

Fragmented clouds

Both Magellanic Clouds lie in the far southern skies, as seen from Earth. To observers south of the Equator, they look like separate parts of the Milky Way.

WHAT YOU CAN SEE

👁 Eye view | 🔭 Binoculars

Viewing notes
To the naked eye, the Large and Small Magellanic Clouds look like separate clumps of the Milky Way. Binoculars reveal features such as the Large Magellanic Cloud's central bar of stars and bright nebulae.

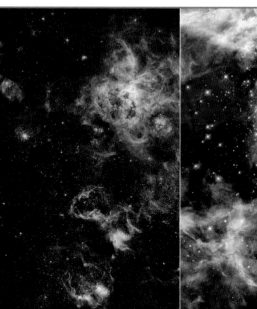

Tarantula Nebula
This large star-forming region is just above the LMC's central bar of stars.

R136 star cluster
This cluster at the heart of the Tarantula Nebula contains the most massive stars known.

Small Magellanic Cloud (SMC)

The SMC is only about 7,000 light-years across. It is not as structured as the LMC, but it is full of star-forming material and brilliant young stars. It may have started life as a small spiral galaxy before being disrupted by the Milky Way's gravity.

NGC 602
This young star cluster has hollowed out a cavern in the surrounding gas clouds.

NGC 346
Radiation from this star cluster sculpts the glowing clouds of gas around it.

Cannibal galaxy

The Milky Way's gravity doesn't just trap smaller galaxies in orbit, it tears them to shreds and gobbles them up. Astronomers think that the huge globular cluster Omega Centauri is the stripped-down core of a previous galaxy.

OMEGA CENTAURI

The **supernova** 1987A in the Large Magellanic Cloud was the brightest exploding star seen for more than **400 years**

An enormous spiral 2.5 million light-years from Earth, the Andromeda galaxy is even bigger than the Milky Way. It is the farthest night-sky object visible with the naked eye.

Giant spiral
From our location in the Milky Way, we see Andromeda (cataloged as M31) at a shallow angle, with dark dust lanes outlining its spiral structure. Like our own galaxy, Andromeda is orbited by several satellites, including bright balls of stars called M32 and NGC 205.

First sightings
The Andromeda galaxy was recorded by medieval Arab astronomers. Its spiral structure, however, wasn't known until the 19th century. Astronomers couldn't agree on its distance or size.

Arab depiction
Astronomer Abd al-Rahman al-Sufi's *Book of Fixed Stars* has the earliest-known descriptions and illustrations of Andromeda.

How far is Andromeda?
Astronomer Edwin Hubble proved that Andromeda lies far beyond our galaxy by looking for unstable stars called Cepheids. The way they vary reveals their true brightnesses; Hubble used these findings to figure out the real distances of these stars.

Pulsating stars
A Cepheid's brightness and size change in a cycle linked to its true luminosity.

The Local Group
The Milky Way and Andromeda are the two biggest galaxies in the Local Group. This group is a cluster of around 50 galaxies spread across about 10 million light-years of space.

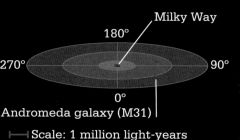

Milky Way

180°

270°   90°

0°
Andromeda galaxy (M31)

Scale: 1 million light-years
LOCATION OF ANDROMEDA

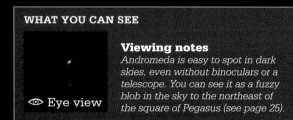

WHAT YOU CAN SEE

Viewing notes
Andromeda is easy to spot in dark skies, even without binoculars or a telescope. You can see it as a fuzzy blob in the sky to the northeast of the square of Pegasus (see page 25).

👁 Eye view

Andromeda and the Milky Way will collide with each other in about

5 billion years

Galaxies galore [Swirls of stars]

The Universe is filled with hundreds of billions of galaxies, each containing stars, gas, and dust. Galaxies come in many shapes and sizes, from complex spirals to huge oval balls of stars called ellipticals to tiny, irregular dwarf galaxies.

Colliding galaxies

Relative to their enormous sizes, galaxies are surprisingly close together in space, separated by distances equal to just a few times their own diameter. As a result, collisions are common. Astronomers think that collisions cause the different galaxy types in Hubble's classification system (see opposite page).

Galaxy clusters

Galaxies are so massive and have such powerful gravity that they are attracted to one another. They tend to form loose groups, such as our own Local Group (see page 98), and bigger clusters of hundreds of galaxies. Groups of dense clusters, known as superclusters, are the largest things in the Universe.

Abell 2218 galaxy cluster
This galaxy cluster, 2 billion light-years away, contains several thousand galaxies.

800,000,000,000:

the number of galaxies in the Universe

Edwin Hubble

In 1925, US astronomer Edwin Hubble proved that galaxies are star systems far beyond the Milky Way. He later invented a system for classifying different types of galaxy.

Edwin Hubble
Hubble not only discovered the true scale of the Universe, he also proved that it is expanding.

Mice galaxies

This stunning pair of spirals is 300 million light-years from Earth. As the two galaxies collided, their spiral arms unwound to create extended tails.

Key: Galaxies

Barred spiral galaxy	
Spiral galaxy	
Giant elliptical galaxy	
Lenticular galaxy	
Irregular galaxy	
Radio galaxy	
Blazar galaxy	
Quasar galaxy	
Seyfert galaxy	

Classifying galaxies

Hubble's system labels galaxies as barred spirals (such as our Milky Way), normal spirals, ball-like ellipticals, armless spirals called lenticulars, or shapeless clouds of gas and stars called irregulars.

BARRED SPIRAL GALAXY (NGC 1300)

SPIRAL GALAXY (M81)

GIANT ELLIPTICAL GALAXY (M87)

LENTICULAR GALAXY (NGC 2787)

IRREGULAR GALAXY (NGC 1427A)

Active galaxies

As a galaxy's central black hole (see pages 60–61) consumes material that drifts close to it, the galaxy can emit bright light and other kinds of radiation. Astronomers have identified four major types of active galaxy, as shown below.

RADIO GALAXY

BLAZAR GALAXY

QUASAR GALAXY

SEYFERT GALAXY

Glorious galaxies

This image, taken by the Hubble Space Telescope, shows faraway galaxies stretching across the Universe. The most distant objects are billions of light-years away, allowing us to look back in time (see pages 104–105). We can see back to when large galaxies, like those we know today, were being formed by galactic collisions.

By looking out across billions of light-years of space, we can begin to understand the structure of our Universe and its possible origins.

Cosmic time machine

Due to the speed of light (see page 49), the farther we look into space, the further back we can see in time. When we look across billions of light-years, we can see a young Universe that has violent quasars (see page 101), bright irregular galaxies, and galactic collisions.

Deepest view
The farthest galaxies we can see are about 13 billion light-years away. We see them in the process of formation, when the Universe was much younger.

Our Universe is

The big bang

Scientists have calculated that our Universe began 13.7 billion years ago in a huge explosion—the big bang. This created all the energy and matter in the Universe, as well as all time and space.

First stars
Eventually, clouds of matter joined to form the first enormous stars.

First galaxies
Galaxies began to form around the black holes left by the first stars.

Ultra-deep field
The most distant Hubble photos see back to this period, 13.2 billion years ago.

Hubble deep field
The first deep images from the Hubble Space Telescope looked back 12 billion years.

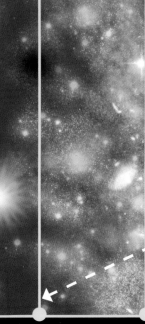

the big bang

The cooling afterglow of the big bang can be seen in the soft glow of radio waves all over the sky.

For 200 million years, there were no stars, and the Universe went through a dark age.

Cosmic expansion

Everything in the Universe is rushing away from everything else. The farther away a galaxy is, the faster it's moving away. Although it's hard to imagine, the Universe is expanding like an inflating balloon!

Tracking back

Cosmic expansion means that at some time in the distant past, everything in the Universe was tightly packed together.

Tight squeeze
In the distant past, galaxies were much closer together.

Big bang

Galaxies expand
In the present-day Universe, galaxies are spaced out.

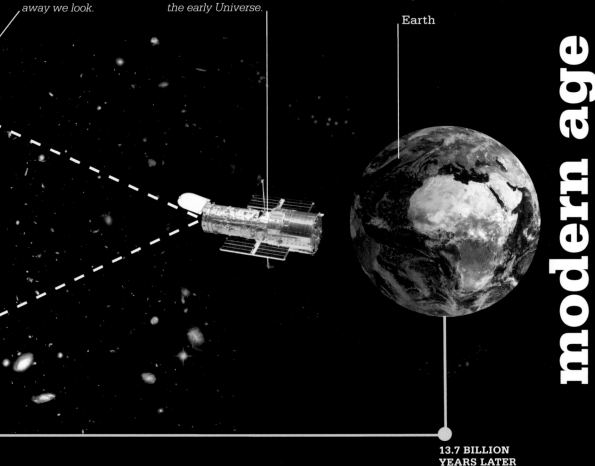

13.7 billion
years old

Active galaxies
We are much more likely to see violent, active galaxies the farther away we look.

Hubble Telescope
Launched in 1990, this orbiting space telescope provides deep views of the early Universe.

Across the Universe
With powerful technology, we can see to the edge of time and space to detect light and radio waves from just after the big bang itself.

Earth

modern age

13.7 BILLION
YEARS LATER

More here

Really, Really Big Questions About Space and Time
by Mark Brake

Hubble deep field
active galaxies
cosmic expansion
ultra-deep field
cosmic microwave background

The Universe: Seasons 1, 2 and 3 (The History Channel)

Visit the Green Bank Telescope in Pocahontas County, West Virgina, the largest fully steerable radio dish in the world, which looks deep into space.

quasar: the bright center of a galaxy, believed to be powered by a massive black hole.

radio wave: a ray with the longest wavelength of all. Radio waves are given out by many objects in space.

Array
A group of telescopes that work together to look at the sky at the same time.

Asterism
A cluster of stars that forms an easily recognized pattern.

Asteroid
A chunk of rock, left over from the birth of the solar system, that orbits the Sun.

Astronomer
A scientist who studies the stars and other objects in space.

Astronomical unit (AU)
A unit equal to the distance between Earth and the Sun, equivalent to 93 million miles (150 million km).

Atmosphere
The layer of gases that surrounds a planet or star. The Earth's atmosphere is called air.

Atom
A tiny particle of matter, consisting of protons, neutrons, and electrons. Atoms are the smallest particles that can take part in chemical reactions.

Aurora borealis
A display of multicolored lights in the sky, caused by particles from the Sun entering Earth's atmosphere. The aurora borealis is also called the northern lights.

Axis
An imaginary straight line from the top of a spinning object such as Earth to its bottom. The object rotates around the axis.

Binary star
A star system consisting of two stars that orbit a common point in space.

Black hole
The superdense collapsed core of a burned-out star that sucks in every object around it in space. Not even light can escape, so a black hole is not visible to the naked eye.

Blazar
An active galaxy that shoots a jet of material straight toward Earth.

Celestial pole
One of two points in the celestial sphere directly above Earth's Poles, around which the sphere seems to spin as Earth rotates.

Celestial sphere
An imaginary shell around the sky, on which the movements of stars and planets can be mapped.

Cepheid
A type of star that pulsates as its size and brightness change over a period of time.

Cluster
A group of stars or galaxies.

Comet
A chunk of frozen gas and dust that travels in an elongated orbit around the Sun. When a comet warms up near the Sun, dust and vapor stream out behind it to produce a spectacular "tail."

Constellation
One of many divisions of the sky described by astronomers, or the patterns of stars within these divisions. There are 88 constellations.

Core
The center of a star or planet, where matter is hottest and most compressed.

Crater
A bowl-shaped depression in a planet's surface, often caused by a meteorite impact.

Dry ice
Carbon dioxide in its solid, frozen form.

Dwarf galaxy
A small galaxy, usually either ball shaped or irregular.

Eclipse
An event in which three astronomical bodies line up with one another—for instance, when the Moon passes in front of the Sun, as seen from Earth, or when the Earth passes between the Sun and the Moon.

Ecliptic
The Sun's path around the celestial sphere each year.

Electron
A lightweight particle with a negative electric charge, found inside an atom.

Elliptical
Shaped like an oval, as a comet's orbit and some galaxies are.

Event horizon
A barrier around a black hole, marking the point where nothing can escape its gravity.

Farside
The side of the Moon that is always turned away from Earth.

Focus
The point in a telescope where light rays come together so that an image can be seen clearly.

Galaxy
A huge structure of stars, gas, and dust, usually in the shape of a spiral, an elliptical ball, or an irregular cloud.

Gas giant
An enormous planet that has a small, solid core surrounded by huge amounts of gas.

Gibbous
Describing the bulging appearance of the Moon when it is larger than a Half Moon but not yet a Full Moon.

Globular cluster
A ball-shaped star cluster containing many thousands of very old, yellowish stars.

Gravity
The force that pulls things toward massive objects such as planets and stars.

Helium
A lightweight gas. Helium is the second-most common element in the Universe.

Hubble Space Telescope
A telescope in orbit around Earth, operated by NASA, that provides many of our best views of space objects.

The surface of the Moon has about the same area as the continent of Africa

Glossary

Hydrogen
The lightest and most common element in the Universe. Hydrogen makes up the bulk of all stars and interstellar gas.

Ice dwarf
A small, icy object that orbits the Sun beyond Neptune.

Infrared
A type of invisible light, produced by objects that are too cool to glow in visible light. Special cameras can use infrared rays to identify objects that cannot be seen with an ordinary camera.

Interstellar
Something that is located or occurring between stars.

Lava tube
A tunnel carved out by molten rock flowing underneath the surface of a planet.

Light-year (ly)
A unit equal to the distance that light can travel in one Earth year in empty space. A light-year is equivalent to approximately 5.9 trillion miles (9.5 trillion km).

Long exposure
A technique used in photography in which the camera's shutter is left open for a long period of time, allowing it to collect more light than the naked eye can detect.

Luminosity
A measure of the energy that a star produces, or the brightness of a star compared to the Sun.

Lunar
Concerning Earth's Moon.

Magnetic field
The invisible area around some planets and other objects in space in which magnetic forces can be felt. A magnetic field affects certain other objects that pass nearby.

Magnitude
A measure of a star's brightness. Apparent magnitude is the brightness of a star as seen from Earth.

Main sequence star
A star in the longest phase of its life cycle, when it shines because it has a stable nuclear reaction. The star moves out of the main sequence when the hydrogen in its core is used up.

Meteor
A piece of space debris that burns up as it passes through the atmosphere around a planet. Meteors vary greatly in size and produce bright lights in the sky as they burn.

Meteorite
A piece of space debris that passes through a planet's atmosphere without burning up. It then crashes on the surface of the planet.

Moon
A large, solid body in orbit around a planet. A moon is a type of natural satellite. Earth's Moon is a small world with no atmosphere and no life.

Nearside
The side of the Moon that is always turned toward Earth.

Nebula
A cloud of gas and dust in interstellar space in which stars are born.

Neutron
A particle with no electrical charge, slightly bigger than a proton. Neutrons are found in the nuclei of all atoms except those of hydrogen.

Neutron star
A tiny, superdense space object formed from the collapsed core of a burned-out star. It is composed of neutrons and spins very fast. Neutron stars are often pulsars.

Nuclear fusion
The process of fusing (joining) the nuclei of atoms. This creates other, heavier atoms and releases a huge amount of energy. Nuclear fusion is the process that makes the Sun burn.

Nucleus
The center of an atom. The plural of *nucleus* is *nuclei*.

Open cluster
A small star cluster containing a few dozen stars that have all formed in the recent past and from the same nebula.

Orbit
The path taken by one object around another under the influence of gravity. The Earth moves in orbit around the Sun.

Phase
The amount of the surface of a planet or moon that reflects the Sun, as seen from another area of space.

Photosphere
The brilliant outer surface of the Sun. It is made of hot gases and gives off almost all of the light that Earth receives from the Sun.

Planet
A body in space that moves in orbit around a star such as the Sun. Planets have no light of their own. They reflect the light of the star that they are orbiting.

Planetary nebula
The gas shell thrown off when a red star dies.

Polaris
The star that appears to be very close to the north celestial pole. Polaris is also called the North Star or the polestar.

Probe
An unmanned robotic spacecraft sent to investigate planets and other space objects up close.

Proton
A positively charged particle, found in the nucleus of an atom.

Pulsar
A neutron star with a powerful magnetic field that emits spinning beams of light, much like a lighthouse does.

Quasar
The bright center of a galaxy, believed to be powered by an enormous black hole.

88 days on Earth

Radiation
A moving electrical and magnetic disturbance that is experienced as light and heat. It is also called electromagnetic radiation.

Radio wave
An electromagnetic wave that is within the range of radio frequencies.

Red giant
A giant star toward the end of its life, which has a relatively low temperature and emits red light.

Reflecting telescope
An instrument that produces a bright, magnified image by collecting light with mirrors.

Refracting telescope
An instrument that produces a bright, magnified image by collecting light with lenses.

Satellite
A small body that orbits a much larger one in space under the influence of the larger body's gravity. Satellites can be natural, such as moons, or artificial.

Shooting star
A bright streak of light in the sky, caused when a meteor enters Earth's atmosphere and burns up.

Solar flare
A sudden eruption of hydrogen gas in the Sun's atmosphere, caused by changes in the Sun's magnetic field.

Solar system
Everything that is held in orbit around a star, such as the Sun, by its gravity. Our solar system includes planets, moons, comets, ice dwarfs, and other objects.

Solar wind
A stream of particles that blows across the solar system from the surface of the Sun.

Star
A huge, glowing ball of gas that gives off its own heat and light. Earth's Sun is a star.

Sunspot
A relatively cool patch on the surface of the Sun that appears dark in comparison to its bright surroundings. Sunspots are caused by the Sun's magnetic field.

Supergiant
An enormous star, with a diameter far larger than Earth's orbit around the Sun.

Supernova
The blast created when a massive star explodes at the end of its normal life. A supernova can outshine all of the other stars in a galaxy.

Ultraviolet
A type of invisible light, produced by objects that are too hot to glow in visible light.

White dwarf
A hot, dense space object, approximately the size of Earth, formed by the core of a burned-out star.

X-ray
A form of radiation produced by stars and hot gas clouds. X-rays are high-frequency waves emitted by some of the most violent processes in the Universe.

Zodiac
The 12 ancient constellations that the Sun passes through each year as it moves along the ecliptic.

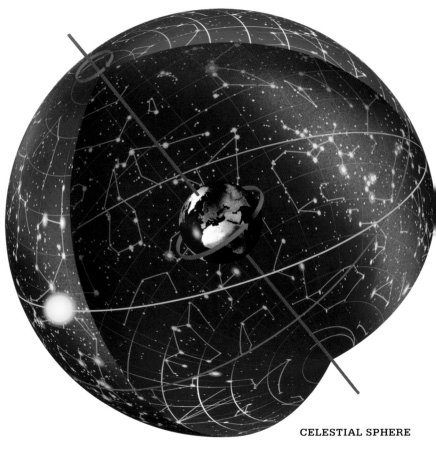

CELESTIAL SPHERE

Index

PHOTOGRAPHY

1: Alex Cherney/Terrastro; 2–3: National Optical Astronomy Observatory; 6: NASA; 7l: David Nunuk/Photo Researchers, Inc.; 7cr: NASA; 7r: Hubble Telescope; 8–9: Kevin Schafer/Getty Images; 10–11: Hubble Telescope; 12l: B.A.E. Inc./Alamy; 12c: Photo Researchers, Inc.; 12r: National Geographic Society/Corbis; 14tr: Photo Researchers, Inc.; 16–17 (eye, binoculars, telescope, and camera icons): Shutterstock; 16–17 (Moon surface): NASA; 16 (Moon): J. Sanford/Photo Researchers, Inc.; 16 (rod cells) Steve Gschmeissner/Science Photo Library; 17tl: Malcolm Park astronomy images/Alamy; 17cl: John Chumack/Photo Researchers, Inc.; 17bl: Hubble Telescope; 17tr: B.A.E. Inc./Alamy; 18tr: National Geographic Society/Corbis; 18bl: Steve Cole/Getty Images; 18br: lamsania/Shutterstock; 19tl, 19clt, 19clb, 19bl: NASA Chandra; 19tr: NASA; 19crt: Hubble Telescope; 19crb: Science Photo Library; 19br: NASA; 20t: Arco Images GmbH/Alamy; 21br: Richard Cummins/Corbis; 23tr: Science Museum; 23b: Babak Tafreshi/Photo Researchers, Inc.; 24bl: HIP/Art Resource; 26cl: Royal Astronomical Society/Photo Researchers, Inc.; 26bl: SPL/Photo Researchers, Inc.; 29tc: Sheila Terry/Science Photo Library; 29tr: J-L Charmet/Photo Researchers, Inc.; 29br: Royal Astronomical Society/Science Photo Library; 30–31: David Nunuk/Photo Researchers, Inc.; 32–33 (meteor shower): Tony & Daphne Hallas/Science Photo Library; 32tl: SPL/Photo Researchers, Inc.; 32c: Photo Researchers, Inc.; 32bl: Detlev van Ravenswaay/Photo Researchers, Inc.; 32br: Mark Garlick/Photo Researchers, Inc.; 33tr: NASA; 33bl: Dieter Spannknebel/Getty Images; 33bc: Detlev van Ravenswaay/Photo Researchers, Inc.; 33br: Louie Psihoyos/Corbis; 34l: European Space Agency/Photo Researchers, Inc.; 34c: National Optical Astronomy Observatory; 34r: Hubble Telescope; 36t: NJIT; 36cl: Claus Lunau/Science Photo Library; 36cr: Daniel J. Cox/Corbis; 37br: EFDA-JET/Photo Researchers, Inc.; 38, 39 (star birth): Hubble Telescope; 39 (star cluster): NASA; 39 (main sequence): Russell Croman/Photo Researchers, Inc.; 39 (red giant), 39 (planetary nebula): Hubble Telescope; 39 (supernova): NASA; 40 (Betelgeuse): Hubble Telescope; 40 (Rigel): John Chumack/Photo Researchers, Inc.; 40 (Orion's belt): NASA; 40 (Horsehead Nebula): National Optical Astronomy Observatory; 40 (Great Orion Nebula): Hubble Telescope; 41br: Eckhard Slawik/Photo Researchers, Inc.; 42 (NGC 6822), 42 (Omega/Swan Nebula): Hubble Telescope; 42 (Trifid Nebula): National Optical Astronomy Observatory; 42 (Lagoon Nebula): European Southern Observatory; 42 (globular cluster M22): NASA; 43br: Jerry Schad/Photo Researchers, Inc.; 44–45, 45cr: Hubble Telescope; 46br: Eckhard Slawik/Photo Researchers, Inc.; 47 (M96): NASA; 47 (M66), 47 (Leo triplet): Hubble Telescope; 47 (Regulus): Russell Croman/Photo Researchers, Inc.; 48–49 (Neptune): Petr84/Shutterstock; 48–49 (Proxima Centauri): NASA; 48 (Moon): Eckhard Slawik/Photo Researchers, Inc.; 48 (Sun): Science Source/Photo Researchers, Inc.; 48b: Culver Pictures, Inc./SuperStock; 49tr: John Chumack/Photo Researchers, Inc.; 49 (Earth): Petr84/Shutterstock; 49 (Oort Cloud): Claus Lunau/FOCI/Bonnier Publications/Photo Researchers, Inc.; 49 (human skull): Pascal Goetgheluck/Photo Researchers, Inc.; 49 (Roman helmet), 49 (Stonehenge): iStockphoto; 49 (dinosaur skull): Marquea/Shutterstock; 50 (North America Nebula): NASA; 50 (Cygnus X-1): David A Hardy, Futures: 50 Years in Space/Science Photo Library; 50 (Crescent Nebula): NASA; 50 (Veil Nebula): National Optical Astronomy Observatory; 50 (Cygnus and Phaeton): The Print Collector/age fotostock; 50 (Albireo): NASA; 51br: Gerard Lodriguss/Photo Researchers, Inc.; 52br: Frank Zullo/Photo Researchers, Inc.; 53 (supergiant): National Optical Astronomy Observatory; 53 (Antares): Sebastian Kaulltzki/Shutterstock; 53 (Pismis 24): NASA; 53 (Cat's Paw Nebula): European Southern Observatory; 54–55: Hubble Telescope; 56 (Orpheus): Fine Art Photographic Library/SuperStock; 56 (Epsilon Lyrae): Galaxy Pictures; 56 (Vega): Chris Butler/Photo Researchers, Inc.; 56 (Cluster M56), 56 (Ring Nebula): Hubble Telescope; 57br: Jerry Schad/Photo Researchers, Inc.; 58 (Nebra sky disk): Wikipedia; 58 (Pleiades): Hubble Telescope; 58 (Crystal Ball Nebula): NASA; 58 (Hyades): Pekka Parviainen/Science Photo Library; 58 (Crab Nebula): Hubble Telescope; 59bl: Frank Zullo/Photo Researchers, Inc.; 60bl: Shutterstock; 60 (pin): Dvarg/Shutterstock; 60 (tanker): Ints Vikmanis/Shutterstock; 61br: Triballum/Shutterstock; 62l: European Southern Observatory; 62c, 62r: NASA; 64 (Sun): Andrea Danti/Shutterstock; 64 (orbiting planets diagram), 64 (Mercury): NASA; 64 (Earth): Shutterstock; 64 (Venus): Luis Stortini Sabor/Shutterstock; 64 (Mars): Sabino Parente/Shutterstock; 65 (Jupiter): NASA; 65 (Uranus): Sabino Parente/Shutterstock; 65 (Saturn): Luis Stortini Sabor/Shutterstock; 65 (Neptune): Sabino Parente/Shutterstock; 64–65 (telescope views at bottom): Galaxypix; 66 (Sun): Science Source/Photo Researchers, Inc.; 66–67 (all planets): Petr84/Shutterstock; 66 (beach ball): Albachiaraa/Shutterstock; 66–67 (baseball): Iraladybird/Shutterstock; 67 (tennis ball): Prism68/Shutterstock; 67 (golf ball): Maniacpixel/Shutterstock; 67 (Ping-Pong ball): Doodle/Shutterstock; 67 (pea): Atoss/Shutterstock; 67 (lentil): Spaxiax/Shutterstock; 67 (rice): Angelo Gilardelli/Shutterstock; 68–69 (Moon phases): Eckhard Slawik/Photo Researchers, Inc.; 69tl: Oorka/Shutterstock; 69tr: Philippe Morel/Photo Researchers, Inc.; 70 (crater from side), 70 (crater from overhead), 71t: NASA; 72tr: Detlev van Ravenswaay/Photo Researchers, Inc.; 72–73 (all others), 74–75: NASA; 76–77 (solar system diagrams): NASA; 76 (Mercury eye view): Larry Landolfi/Photo Researchers, Inc.; 76 (Mercury telescope view): Galaxypix; 76 (Venus eye view): Babak Tafreshi/Photo Researchers, Inc.; 76 (Venus telescope view): Galaxypix; 76bl, 76c: NASA; 76br: Galaxypix; 77t: Babak Tafreshi/Photo Researchers, Inc.; 77r: NASA; 77cl: Stocktrek Images, Inc./Alamy; 77cm: NASA; 77bl: Don P. Mitchell; 78 (Mars eye view), 78 (Mars telescope view): Hubble Telescope; 78 (rover), 78 (icy planet): NASA; 78 (river valley): European Southern Observatory; 78b: NASA; 79tr: Mary Evans Picture Library/Alamy; 79cl: Detlev van Ravenswaay/Photo Researchers, Inc.; 79cr, 80–81 (Jupiter), 80t: NASA; 80c: Hubble Telescope; 80bl: NASA; 81 (Jupiter eye view): Laurent Laveder/Photo Researchers, Inc.; 81 (Jupiter telescope view): Galaxypix; 81 (Callisto), 81 (Ganymede), 81 (Europa), 81 (Io): NASA; 81tr, 81br: Hubble Telescope; 82–83 (Saturn): NASA; 83 (all): Hubble Telescope; 84–85 (solar system diagrams): NASA; 84tl: Science Source/Photo Researchers, Inc; 84tc: Royal Astronomical Society/Science Photo Library; 84tr: Victor Habbick Visions/Photo Researchers, Inc.; 84r: California Association for Research in Astronomy/Photo Researchers, Inc.; 84 (Uranus telescope view): Galaxypix; 85tc, 85tr: NASA; 85 (changing weather): Hubble Telescope; 85 (Neptune telescope view): Galaxypix; 86–87 (all): NASA; 89br: with special authorization of the city of Bayeux/Bridgeman Art Library; 90l: NASA; 92–93 (Milky Way), 92br: European Southern Observatory; 93tl: David Nunuk/Photo Researchers, Inc.; 93tc: Babak Tafreshi/Photo Researchers, Inc.; 93 (eye view): B.A.E. Inc./Alamy; 93 (telescope view): European Southern Observatory; 93bl, 93br: NASA; 94–95: Luc Perrot; 96–97 (Milky Way): European Southern Observatory; 96tc, 96tr: Hubble Telescope; 96 (eye view): European Southern Observatory; 96 (binocular view): NOAO/AURA/NSF/S.Points, C.Smith & MCELS team; 97tl: European Southern Observatory; 97tcl, 97tcr, 97tr: Hubble Telescope; 97 (Omega Centauri): European Southern Observatory; 98tl: Bodleian Library; 98cl, 98cr: European Southern Observatory; 98bl: William Attard McCarthy; 98–99 (Andromeda), 100–101 (Mice galaxies), 100bl: Hubble Telescope; 101tl: Emilio Segrè Visual Archives/American Institute of Physics/Photo Researchers, Inc.; 101 (center column): Hubble Telescope; 101tr: NASA; 101crt: Jodrell Bank/Science Photo Library; 101crb: NASA/ESA/STSCI/J. Bahcall/Princeton IAS/Science Photo Library; 101br: National Optical Astronomy Observatory; 102–103, 104tr: Hubble Telescope; 105tc: Victor De Schwanberg/Science Photo Library; 105tr: Richard Kail/Science Photo Library.

ARTWORK

7cl, 14–15 (all others), 17 (all other icons), 20 (all others), 21 (all others), 22 (all), 23 (all others), 24¬–25 (all others), 26–27 (all others), 28–29 (all others), 36–37 (Sun cross section), 40 (all others), 41 (star map), 42 (all others), 43 (star map), 45 (all others), 46 (star map), 47 (all others), 50 (all others), 51 (star map), 52 (star map), 53 (all others), 56 (all others), 57 (star map), 58 (all others), 59 (star map), 60–61 (all others), 68–69 (all others), 70–71 (all others), 78–79 (all others), 80br, 84–85 (all others), 88–89 (all others), 90 (all others), 92–93 (all others), 96tl, 98bc, 101 (all icons), 104–105b, 108: Tim Brown/Pikaia Imaging; 18 (telescopes): Tim Loughhead/Precision Illustration; all other artwork: Scholastic.

COVER

Front cover: Louie Psihoyos/Science Faction/Corbis. Back cover: (star maps) Tim Brown/Pikaia Imaging; (northern lights) Chris Madeley/Photo Researchers, Inc.; (computer screen) Manaemedia/Dreamstime.

Credits and acknowledgments